New Wave King

The Cinematography of Laszlo Kovacs, ASC

New Wave King

The Cinematography of Laszlo Kovacs, ASC

A collection from the pages
of *American Cinematographer* magazine
and journalist Bob Fisher

Compiled and edited
by Ray Zone

Foreword by
Vilmos Zsigmond, ASC

First Published in 2002

10 9 8 7 6 5 4 3 2 1

Printed in the United States of America

Library of Congress Cataloguing in Publication Data
Zone, Ray, ed.
New Wave King: The cinematography of Laszlo Kovacs, ASC
1. Cinematography. 2. Motion Pictures.

ISBN 0-935578-19-6

ASC Press
1782 North Orange Drive
Hollywood, California 90028

Acknowledgements

With this collection of articles from the pages of *American Cinematographer* magazine and elsewhere, we examine the films of Laszlo Kovacs, ASC.

This volume is the second in a series of books from the ASC Press on contemporary cinematographers, film formats, genres and classic cameramen from cinema history.

Thanks are due to Jim McCullaugh, intrepid publisher of *American Cinematographer*; Martha Winterhalter for excellent art direction; Marion Gore and Tim Humphrey for sterling labors with graphic design; Rachael Bosley for editing; gaffer extraordinaire Richard "Aggie" Aguilar for sharing his memories; Peter Sorel for photography; and Laszlo Kovacs for giving his valuable time and talents in the interest of this historical record.

Thanks are also due to the authors whose writing is collected here, notably Vilmos Zsigmond, Les Paul Robley, Randy Lofficier, Richard Patterson, Jon Silberg and especially Bob Fisher, without whom this volume would not have been possible. Bob contributed most of the articles in this book. He is omnipresent in the motion-picture industry and an illustrious champion of cinematography who has served as the very voice of the cinematographer for many years. This volume is dedicated to him, with gratitude.

New Hollywood residents Laszlo Kovacs (left) and Vilmos Zsigmond, holding 16mm Bolex cameras, in 1959.

Foreword

My Name is Not Laszlo

by

Vilmos Zsigmond, ASC

The first time I met Laszlo Kovacs was at the film school in Budapest, almost fifty years ago. When the revolution came in 1956, Laszlo and I ran into each other on the street. I was thinking about putting together a documentary. I said, "Laszlo, we should get a camera. We should record some of these events." I had already graduated from the film school, and Laszlo was still going there. We went to the school and found an Arriflex. We grabbed it and went out into the streets, and we shot a lot of footage together. It showed the ruins of Budapest, the tanks going up and down the streets, people running and cannons firing.

After three days it became difficult and dangerous to shoot, because if they caught you they would kill you right on the spot. They even shot a still photographer and took him away. We had to hide and shoot from the second floor of a building, through a hole created by a rocket. We had to be very careful. We had just a couple of standard lenses on the camera and a battery. When we finished our work, we couldn't develop the film because a strike was happening. We didn't know what to do with the film. We wanted to turn it in to the film studio, but they said, "No, no, don't turn it in. The Russians will take it away. Keep it."

A couple of days later, after a big meeting at the studio, they were looking for people to take the film out of there, out to the West. Not many people wanted to go. The cameramen in Hungary didn't want to leave their jobs, even with the Russian occupation.

I don't know why I got it in my mind to get out of there. I was thinking, "What should I do?" I lived then in a tiny little room with a broken window. It had been a maid's room. It was November, and it was cold and rainy. My father was in Morocco, and I thought about going to visit him to get some work experience. I had learned everything I could in Hungary. I needed to get some experience in a foreign land.

So I volunteered to take the film out of the country. By accident, I ran into Laszlo in the street. I said, "Laszlo, do you want to get out of here?"

"Where?" said Laszlo.

"Just out of here, anywhere," I said.

"Yeah," Laszlo said. "I've been thinking about it."

I brought Laszlo to the studio, and there were three of us who decided we would take the film — not only our film, but also the film other students had shot. It had to get to the West. We knew that the Russians were going to come to the studio and find the film.

Later on, in 1961, CBS used our footage in a half-hour documentary called "Revolt in Hungary."

Laszlo and I came to America in different ways because we got separated somehow. I went to New York for a year, and then to Hollywood, where I found that nobody would hire me. Laszlo worked at a maple-syrup factory in Vermont, then went to Seattle and found work in a film lab. I worked at all kinds of jobs. I even did home photography, which was absolutely miserable.

After we met up again in Hollywood, Laszlo and I would work for each other on TV commercials. We worked just for experience. Then we did those cheap features on 16mm, like *Incredibly Strange Creatures.* We did a movie with Ray Dennis Steckler called *Wild Guitar*, with Arch Hall Jr. Joe Mascelli was the director of photography, Laszlo was the gaffer and I was the camera operator. While we were shooting that film, a representative from Eastman Kodak came to visit. "We're looking for future cameramen," he said. It gave us encouragement.

Laszlo got into better filmmaking a little bit sooner than I did. I did commercials, and Laszlo ended up doing biker movies. Then he did *Easy Rider* and was asked to do *Five Easy Pieces.* When Peter Fonda was going to direct *The Hired Hand*, Laszlo recommended me to him. After *The Hired Hand*, I did a Universal Picture called *Red Sky at Morning.* Laszlo did *A Cold Day in the Park*, an early Altman picture. When Laszlo couldn't shoot *McCabe & Mrs. Miller* because of another commitment, he told Altman to take me. I met Altman, who trusted Laszlo's opinion and hired me.

Laszlo and I have the same background, and we learned so much from our instructors. When we came to Hollywood, these new, young directors came up from nowhere, just like the Italian Neorealists and the filmmakers of the French New Wave, or *nouvelle vague.* Those were the kinds of films these guys wanted to do in America — they didn't want slick, old Hollywood photography, but something really good and realistic. People were looking for a more documentary style.

And Laszlo and I knew it. The directors said, "It doesn't matter which one of the Hungarians you get, because either one will deliver you a good movie." Our styles are pretty similar; they're based on good lighting and good camerawork.

You know, personality has a lot to do with Laszlo's success, too. He has a very charming personality, and he would charm the hell out of all those people. Laszlo really is a nice guy, a good-looking, nice guy who could have been a movie star. He has always been likable. I've never met anyone who dislikes him. I've been friends with him for fifty years, and we've never had an argument. We never get mad at each other. There is no way to get mad at Laszlo!

Laszlo and I had to study to become cameramen. Now people call us artists. It's a nice compliment, and we both accept it. But the reality is that we worked very hard to become artists.

Contents

Director Richard Rush (left) and Kovacs filming *The Savage Seven* (1968).

American Neorealist: Laszlo Kovacs and the New Hollywood

An Introduction

by

Ray Zone

In the 1960s a new form of audience for the movies evolved in America. It was a new generation of filmgoers, literate and passionately articulate about the movies, who had been frequenting art-house cinemas for a decade. At these art houses, which were centered in large urban areas or adjacent to universities across America, postwar Italian Neorealist motion pictures by directors such as Roberto Rossellini and Vittorio De Sica were standard fare. Young filmgoers eagerly watched movies like Rossellini's *Open City* and De Sica's *The Bicycle Thief* and *Umberto D* for their raw social realism and their accurate depictions of the world in which they were made.

Those films were a marked contrast to the slickness of most Hollywood product of the 1950s, and they employed location shooting rather than studio sets and documentary-style photography. In the essay "De Sica: Metteur en Scene," French film critic André Bazin defined the primary characteristics of Neorealist cinema: "The performance calls upon the actor to *be* before expressing himself" and dispenses with "the expressionism of traditional acting." Furthermore, "the natural setting is to the artificial set what the amateur actor is to the professional."

Most importantly, Bazin wrote that Neorealism challenged cinematic artifice and the montage theories of Sergei Eisenstein. "The assemblage of the film must never add anything to the existing reality," Bazin wrote. Long takes and an absence of dissolves and fades characterize Neorealist cinema.

As the 1960s began, the French New Wave blew into art-house cinemas with François Truffaut's *The 400 Blows.* A few years earlier, in an article in *Cahiers du Cinéma* titled "A Certain Tendency in French Cinema," Truffaut had introduced the manifesto *la politique des auteurs* (the author's politics or world view), which was later called the "auteur theory" by

American film critic Andrew Sarris. Truffaut argued that a film "should ideally be a medium of personal artistic expression, and the best films are therefore those which most clearly bear their makers' 'signature.'"

Truffaut was one of several younger critics who wrote for *Cahiers du Cinéma* and launched the French New Wave. Also in the group were Jean-Luc Godard, Claude Chabrol, Jacques Rivette and Eric Rohmer. The second principle the critics espoused was a rejection of montage, and by the 1960s they had all begun to put their theories into practice by making films.

The standard-bearer for the *nouvelle vague* was Godard, who, with his 1959 film *Breathless,* attempted to smash the artistic boundaries of conventional cinema. "[It] was the sort of film where anything goes," wrote Godard. "That was what it was all about.... I also wanted to give the feeling that the techniques of filmmaking had just been discovered or experienced for the first time."

The cinematographer most responsible for the French New Wave was Raoul Coutard, who shot *Breathless* in black-and-white and entirely handheld, using the compact Eclair Cameflex camera. Working with low film sensitivity, Coutard created an innovative and portable bounce-lighting system for shooting in the narrow confines of an actual hotel room that enabled the actors to move freely about during the shot.

A limited budget accounts for much of the cinematic innovation in *Breathless.* In the book *Screencraft: Cinematography*, Coutard observes that a problem "in trying to define the *nouvelle vague* is that so much of what we did in aesthetic terms was determined by lack of money rather than artistic intention." French soundstages charged everything at a 300-percent mark-up. "We had no choice," Coutard said. "We were forced to take to the streets, and that affected everything — how the actors performed, how the films were shot."

As the 1960s dawned in America, young filmmakers such as Richard Rush, Peter Bogdanovich, Francis Ford Coppola, Dennis Hopper, Bob Rafelson and Martin Scorsese were soaking up every Italian Neorealist and French New Wave film they could take in. At the same time, a counter-cultural revolution was beginning to take place.

One of the most complete histories of 1970s filmmaking is Peter Biskind's *Easy Riders, Raging Bulls: How the Sex-Drugs-And-Rock 'N' Roll Generation Saved Hollywood.* "In America," Biskind writes, "real innovation was coming not so much from feature directors as from the practitioners of *cinéma vérité* like Richard Leacock, D.A. Pennebaker and the Maysles brothers, who had developed cheap, lightweight equipment that enabled a whole generation to take to the streets to capture a reality that was rapidly becoming more fantastical than anything springing from the febrile brow of even the most inventive screenwriters."

By the mid-Sixties, the revolution was going full-bore in Hollywood. "As America burned," writes Biskind, "Hell's Angels gunned their bikes down Sunset Boulevard while girls danced topless in the street to the music of the Doors booming from the clubs that lined the Strip."

Laszlo Kovacs had been in Hollywood just a few years when all this began to take place. After emigrating from Hungary in 1958, he had begun to work as a gaffer and cameraman on low-budget exploitation features such as *The Incredibly Strange Creatures Who Stopped Living and Became Mixed-Up Zombies* and *Kiss Me Quick.*

Approached by the young director Richard Rush, Kovacs began filming a series of biker films — *Hell's Angels on Wheels, The Savage Seven* and *The Rebel Rousers* — as well as *Psych-Out,* a film about hippies shot on location on Haight Street in San Francisco. Working with low budgets and short shooting schedules of three to four weeks, Kovacs was his own operator, and he became adept with a handheld Arri IIC camera and rack focus using a zoom telephoto lens.

Biskind attributes the Hollywood New Wave of the 1970s to the young directors and makes little mention of cinematographers. But in the October 4, 1971, issue of *Take One* magazine, writer Michael Goodwin properly restored some of the credit to where it belonged: "Light and shadow, color intensity, focus, depth of field, composition; these are the variables. Frequently the director will have a clear idea of how he wants these things to function, but it is the cameraman alone who achieves them." Noting that "Laszlo Kovacs' cinematography communicates ideas and emotions," Goodwin called Kovacs "the only American cinematographer who can be mentioned in the same breath with Raoul Coutard." For both Coutard and Kovacs, economic necessity was the mother of cinematic invention. For Kovacs, rack focus was essential for filming motorcycles from a moving vehicle, as well as for shooting long takes of actors without having to cover reverse angles.

Goodwin continued, "Richard Rush was one of the first directors to really use rack focus." Rush is quoted: "If you want to improvise, you have to be able to stage your scenes in terms of long, continuous passages that you don't have to cover. Laszlo and I worked with telephoto lenses and ended up in the critical focus style where we start in a close-up, go into a two-shot, glimpse the room for a second, and go back into a close-up—all without editing." In keeping with the artistic tenets of *nouvelle vague,* the cinematic artifice of montage is avoided and the realism of the scene is underscored because events elapse in natural time.

By the time Kovacs was approached by Dennis Hopper and asked to photograph *Easy Rider,* he had become a master of cinematic economy using the telephoto zoom, filming with a style that was both highly pragmatic and aesthetically pleasing. Filmed on the road over a period of 12 weeks, *Easy Rider* was carefully crafted *cinéma vérité* produced by Kovacs with minimal lighting and a single camera. "Laszlo Kovacs is the greatest telephoto-lens operator in the world," Hopper recently told *American Cinematographer.* "*Easy Rider* would never have been made without him. All of the shots using the telephoto are pure Laszlo magic."

The tremendous international success of *Easy Rider* made the studios sit up and take note. "The real legacy of *Easy Rider*," writes Greg Merritt in the book *Celluloid Mavericks: A History of American Independent Film*, "is that it officially ushered in the American New Wave of small, personal, frequently challenging movies."

Director Bob Rafelson was a knowledgeable film buff who hired Kovacs to photograph *Five Easy Pieces*, an intimate drama that was filmed on location while traveling up the West Coast to Canada. "If you asked me who my favorite European cinematographer was," says Rafelson, "it would be Raoul Coutard. I had seen all of his movies before I started working with Laszlo."

Though it had a larger budget — approximately $1 million — Kovacs photographed *Five Easy Pieces* in the *vérité* style in which he was so fluent, using minimal cast and crew. In 1972 Kovacs worked with Rafelson on another intimate drama shot entirely on location. *The King of Marvin Gardens* is Kovacs' *Breathless.*

As in *Breathless*, much of the action in *The King of Marvin Gardens* takes place in a real hotel room. To make matters even more challenging for the cinematographer, Rafelson elected to film in a room on the tenth floor, eliminating the possibility of source lighting through outside windows. The director remarks, "When you shoot on location — and this was already part of the movement of the late Sixties and early Seventies — you are often going to be put into confined quarters. I happen to like it."

Unlike the bounce lighting utilized by Coutard, Kovacs rigged, in Rafelson's words, "some kind of a gizmo to hang lights from the ceiling" so that the actors could freely move about during a shot. Just as Godard did with *Breathless*, Rafelson insisted on long takes, including one shot that lasted seven minutes.

Though Rafelson generally eschewed camera movement on *Five Easy Pieces* and *The King of Marvin Gardens*, the zoom lens was essential for Kovacs to film in naturalistic time. "Laszlo made the zoom invisible," says Rafelson. "Sometimes in interiors, we would be using tracking shots, and to maintain a certain kind of head size Laszlo would use a track and a zoom simultaneously."

By 1975, New Wave filmmaking had changed Hollywood. Along with the new directors, young cinematographers such as Vilmos Zsigmond, Conrad Hall, William Fraker, John Alonzo, Owen Roizman, Victor Kemper and Haskell Wexler were established with Kovacs at the top rank in Hollywood. Eventually all of them were invited to join the American Society of Cinematographers. The era of the blockbuster was about to begin.

As of this writing, Kovacs has filmed more than 60 motion pictures in almost every conceivable genre. His primary concern in narrative cinematography remains human emotion. "What makes Laszlo so special?" Michael Goodwin mused in 1971. "A very simple and exceedingly rare thing: he is aware of the emotional and ideological implications of his technical operations. Putting it another way, his shots mean something."

An atmospheric shot featuring Jack Nicholson in *Psych-Out* (1968).

References:

Bazin, André. "De Sica. Metteur en Scene," *What is Cinema? Vol. I.* University of California Press: Berkeley and Los Angeles, 1971.

Biskind, Peter. *Easy Riders, Raging Bulls: How the Sex-Drugs-and-Rock 'n' Roll Generation Saved Hollywood,* Simon & Schuster: New York, 1998.

Bondanella, Peter. *Italian Cinema From Neorealism to the Present.* 3rd Edition. Continuum: New York, 2001.

Ettedgui, Peter. *Cinematography Screencraft* . Focal Press: London, 1998.

Goodwin, Michael. "Camera: Laszlo Kovacs." *Take One.* October 4, 1971.

Haberski, Raymond J. *It's Only a Movie! Films and Critics in American Culture.* University Press of Kentucky: Lexington, 2001.

Merritt, Greg. *Celluloid Mavericks: A History of American Independent Film.* Thunder's Mouth Press: New York, 2000.

Milne, Tom, Ed. *Godard on Godard,* Secker & Warburg: London, 1972.

PHOTO: SUZANNE HANOVER

Kovacs filming *Jack Frost* (1998) on location in 1998, operating a Super Technocrane with a hooded monitor.

1

Conversation with Laszlo Kovacs, ASC

by

Bob Fisher

Laszlo Kovacs, ASC was born and raised in a small farming village in Hungary about 60 miles from Budapest. During the Nazi occupation of Hungary, his mother was friendly with a woman who ran a weekend cinema in the village. The cinema only showed propaganda films from Germany. The 16mm films were projected on a sheet that hung in a school auditorium. Kovacs was 11 years old when he volunteered to distribute flyers advertising new films. In return, he was given a front row seat. The films were a magical escape from reality. In 1945, the Russians replaced the Nazis, and after that most of the films shown at the village cinema came from communist countries.

Kovacs' parents were farmers. They sent him to school in Budapest at the age of 16, hoping he would become a doctor or engineer. He often skipped math and science classes, preferring to spend his days at a local cinema. When he heard about the Academy of Drama and Film in Budapest, he applied to the program and was accepted in 1952. There were American films in the archives, and students were allowed to watch them on Saturdays. Kovacs still recalls the thrill of sitting on the floor of a jam-packed screening room and watching *Citizen Kane.* "It had a stunning affect on everyone, especially the lighting by Gregg Toland," he says. "It changed my visual vocabulary."

Fate intervened in 1956, when there was a spontaneous uprising that threatened to topple the Communist regime. Kovacs met Vilmos Zsigmond on a street corner, and together they watched the events unfold. Zsigmond had recently graduated from the film school. They decided it was important to record those events for posterity and liberated a camera and film from the university. The revolt failed when Russian troops and tanks surged into Budapest and crushed the dissidents. Kovacs and Zsigmond left the country carrying some 30,000 feet of documentary film.

Kovacs subsequently shot such films as *Easy Rider; Five Easy Pieces; The King of Marvin Gardens; Shampoo; Slither; Paper Moon; New York, New York; What's Up, Doc?; The Runner Stumbles; Ghostbusters; Mask; Copycat* and *My Best Friend's Wedding.*

This interview was conducted for the British magazine *Cuts* in 1998, after Kovacs was honored with the CamerImage Golden Frog Lifetime Achievement Award.

***Cuts:* Weren't you and Vilmos nearly captured when you left Hungary in 1956?**

Kovacs: We ran into a Russian army unit in a village near the border, so we hid the film in a cornfield and walked into the village, pretending to be locals. The Russians had us against a wall with our arms raised. They were questioning and searching us and some other people. That's when I remembered that I had hidden some black-and-white negatives [of stills] that I'd taken during the revolution in the leg of my ski pants. I had eight to 10 rolls of film hidden there. Vilmos was standing on my right side, and I whispered that I had the film. We didn't know what to do. This officer who was searching us looked right into my eyes, and then he started searching me. He stopped at my knees and just looked at me. That's how close we came to being discovered. Later that night we picked up the film that we had hidden in the cornfield and crossed the border into Austria.

How did you come to the United States?

Kovacs: Different countries set up quotas for political refugees. The United States said they would take 60,000. Vilmos and I had plans to go to Hollywood. We saw pictures of a station wagon and thought it would be a great production car. We had a definite plan to get some equipment and a car and rent ourselves out to producers.

But first you made one trip back into Hungary. Why?

Kovacs: Vilmos and I had girlfriends who were supposed to meet us in Vienna. We checked every morning with the Red Cross for new arrivals. One night I told Vilmos I was going back to Hungary to get the girls out. It was December 6 or 7 in 1956. Vilmos was going to meet us in a little Austrian village on the other side of the border exactly a week from the day I left. I found out from my girlfriend's mother that she was already in Vienna. Vilmos' girlfriend lived in a beautiful old medieval town that had a theater, where she performed. I hired a cab. It was a three- or four-hour drive, and the driver wasn't anxious to go because things were still very bad, but I had a pocketful of Hungarian money so he finally agreed.

I found Vilmos' girlfriend, Elizabeth. We went back to Budapest to get Vilmos' Uncle John, who was about 76 years old. There was another old man, Uncle Gustav, who came with us. We waited until about 11 o'clock at night, until everything was quiet. Then we headed for the border. You could see the gleam of the sky from this little Austrian village. It was very quiet. I remember seeing a faint light from the church in a cemetery on the border. We headed that way. When we got close to the cemetery, I told everyone to begin crawling very quietly. Uncle John had a little knapsack on his back, and it was making a loud, clanking noise. He was carrying a candelabra and some silver wrapped in newspaper. Suddenly a flashlight came on, and two Hungarian border guards were telling us to stand up. Elizabeth, Uncle John and Uncle Gustav were crying, and a guard was telling us we were breaking the law. We knew they could shoot us right there and nobody would care.

Uncle Gustav started explaining that he was going to find his son and bring him back. He showed them his watch, but they weren't interested. So he reached into his pocket and took out some money; he said it was his life's savings. One of the guards took the money and told us to go. We were less than 50 yards from the cemetery, and we started walking in that direction. It was very quiet. I can still close my eyes and see the rusted barbed wire at the entrance of the cemetery. As we stepped over it, I shouted for everyone to run. We started zigzagging through the tombstones, and we could hear those two guys laughing as loudly as they could, like it was the funniest thing they'd ever seen. They could have shot us. We got to the church, and there was a little walkway lined with chestnut trees that led to the main street in the village. We got to the tavern where we were supposed to meet Vilmos at 1 a.m. The door opened, and Vilmos stepped out and told me I was late.

What happened after you finally got to the United States?

Kovacs: We arrived at Camp Kilmer in New Jersey, which was converted into a huge processing center for Hungarian émigrés. We tried to explain that we were camera operators — that's what cinematographers were called in Hungary. We said we wanted to go to Hollywood. No one knew what a camera operator did, and they said Los Angeles was a terrible place.

The rules were that a family would agree to sponsor each refugee for a year so we wouldn't go on welfare. They found a family where the man was a professional photographer; they said I could work for him processing film and making prints. It was in Canton in upstate New York. They put me on a train, and I traveled for two days. We finally arrived in this little town. I began to get a sense of how big this country was compared to Hungary.

What happened after you arrived?

Kovacs: There was a welcoming committee at the station. I didn't speak a word of English and, of course, they didn't speak Hungarian. But people were very friendly — I got hugged by everyone! My sponsor and his wife had an English-Hungarian dictionary, and he tried to explain that he had a Polaroid camera, and for a dollar or two you could get your picture taken in his studio. I worked there for a while. One day he took me out to the forest in a pickup truck with a couple of small, open barrels. He kept trying to explain that we were going to get maple syrup from trees. There were huge plastic bags full of liquid tapped into the trees. My job was taking the bags off the trees and handing them to him. He poured it into the barrels until they were full. My weekly salary was $60, but I had to give his wife $40 for room and board. He told me tax was $12, so I had exactly $8 in my pocket every week.

What were your feelings at that point in your life?

Kovacs: I was grateful for the help I got, but honestly, I felt my life had come to a terrible dead end. I wrote to my mother, but I didn't tell her about the grim situation I was in. She wrote back and told me that my cousin David was in Seattle. I wrote to him, and then we spoke by phone. He described Seattle as paradise; David had finished medical school, and his sponsor was helping him to get an internship at a hospital. The following day, his sponsor called and asked if I wanted to come to Seattle. He offered me an airplane ticket, but I took the bus because I wanted to see the country. The trip took seven days, and it was a mesmerizing experience that left me with so many impressions.

What happened after you reached Seattle?

Kovacs: By then I could speak a little English. My cousin's sponsor was a pilot for United Airlines, and he had a beautiful home at the edge of a lake. You could look out the window and see this incredible snowcapped mountain. After breakfast the next morning, he started quizzing me about my profession. 'Film' was the only word we both understood. He looked in the Yellow Pages, and the next day we drove to every film laboratory in the phone book. One person after another said there were no openings. At the last place, an older gentleman said, 'Okay, you start tomorrow.' It was a 16mm black-and-white lab that processed kinescope film and newsreels for Channel 5, KING-TV, in Seattle. I was absolutely thrilled. It eventually became Alpha Cine Labs and was acquired by Les Davis.

What made you decide to go to Los Angeles?

Kovacs: I worked at the lab for almost two years and got to know a lot of people at the TV station. We were working day and night. It was all color reversal film. I was having a great time, but Vilmos and I kept in touch by mail, and we never gave up on the idea of taking our chances in Hollywood. He was working for a color lab in Evanston, Illinois. I dreaded telling Les I was leaving. He told me there were too many people and not enough jobs in Los Angeles, but he wished me the best of luck and said I would always be welcome.

Did you ever go back?

Kovacs: I didn't see Les again until 1975, when he asked me to be the keynote speaker at the Seattle Film Festival. I already had some credits by then — my latest film was *Shampoo.* I was answering questions at the podium, and I saw one gentleman, way in the back, raising his hand. He was obviously a refugee from India or some other country in the Middle East. He asked, "When did you become an American?" I thought before answering, "When I dreamt in English for the first time." I also told him that before, I'd dreamt in black-and-white, but now I dreamt in color *and* black-and-white.

What did you do when you arrived in Los Angeles in 1958?

Kovacs: Vilmos had a classmate, Joseph Zsuffa, who was a director. He had a wonderful short story that he wanted to film, *The Blue of the Sky.* I was the entire crew. We didn't have much light and couldn't afford a generator. We started shooting in Los Angeles and finished in Yosemite.

Did you and Vilmos ever consider making a movie about your lives?

Kovacs: When I was shooting *For Pete's Sake* with Peter Yates, I told him our story, and he thought it would make an interesting movie. We actually got a bunch of people together who had shared our experiences, and we made a tape-recording of us telling our stories. I don't know what happened to that tape.

What happened after Zsuffa's film?

Kovacs: We faced the cold reality of having to find jobs. It looked hopeless, but we didn't see it that way. We were thinking if it doesn't happen today or tomorrow, maybe next week or next month. We were very confident. There was no choice. This was always more than a profession; it was my life. I couldn't imagine doing anything else.

Looking back, how long have you felt that way?

Kovacs: I think I've felt that way since I was 11 years old and sat in the front row watching those 16mm propaganda movies. It was like somebody opened a window on a different world. I owe a lot to Gyorgy Illes (head of the cinematography department at the Budapest film school), who taught us how important it is to study all the arts. In my first semester he had me draw charcoal portraits, and he taught us to see forms, light, tones, textures and all of the things you instinctively use in cinematography. We studied music, literature, art history and architecture.

What were the milestones for you early in your career?

Kovacs: All of the experiences Vilmos and I got working on low-budget films in the 1960s were very important. We knew we weren't making the world's best films, but we were learning. Vilmos and I discovered Haskell Wexler's early movies and got in touch with him. His work was a breakthrough because it was very different than the studio pictures. John Cassavettes was also making interesting films. I did a lot of experimenting on low-budget exploitation films made strictly as the second feature for drive-ins. I shot a lot of biker movies before *Easy Rider.*

This is the 30th anniversary of the making of *Easy Rider.* Did you have any idea it would become a classic?

Kovacs: None of us had that idea. The only thing we were hoping for was that it would be better than the standard drive-in programming! We had a really great time shooting it because of Dennis Hopper, Peter Fonda and Jack Nicholson. We had a lot of freedom even though we were working with a tiny budget. It was a very tightly organized production, and we definitely felt we were making a good movie.

We prepared as carefully as we could for about three weeks. We got into a station wagon and drove from Los Angeles to New Orleans to scout for locations with the right visual backgrounds. Dennis had a lot of ideas about places in New Mexico and Arizona — Taos, Santa Fe and the Painted Desert. We also shot a lot on the streets of Flagstaff, including the main-title sequence, and at locations in Los Angeles. We packed everything in two five-ton trucks. One truck was for the bikes, and the other was for all of the camera and lighting equipment. The cast and crew traveled in station wagons, and my camera car was a 1968 Chevy convertible, which I picked for its shocks. We put the top down and put a 4-by-4 sheet of plywood on the back. With a High Hat, I could swing the camera from left to right. We used a kind of sign language that was very simple: we pointed and waved. There were no PAs, ADs, police or two-way radios.

Sony recently restored several of your films from that period. What kind of response do they get from young people?

Kovacs: Sony rescued *Easy Rider, Five Easy Pieces, The King of Marvin Gardens* and *Shampoo* from oblivion. I've gone to film festivals with some of the restored prints.

They showed *Easy Rider* at a festival in Flagstaff, and there were about 400 people in the audience, including would-be cinematographers, directors and screenwriters. There were also people in their seventies. I asked how many had seen the film in a theater, and about 10 people raised their hands. But about 70 percent had seen it on TV or on a VCR. I've probably seen the film 40 times, and every time I watch it I discover something I hadn't noticed before. The spirit of *Easy Rider* is captivating. It was a very emotional experience for me to see that this 30-year-old film could still move people.

When did you actually get into the guild?

Kovacs: *Easy Rider* had a major impact on my career. I was a member of NABET [the National Association of Broadcast Employees and Technicians] when I shot it because I still couldn't get into the guild. I didn't have an agent. Producers and directors would call about films, and I'd have to say, 'I'm not in the IA.' They'd say, 'Don't worry, we'll take care of it.' Finally, Robert Altman directed *A Cold Day in a Park* in Vancouver, Canada, because he wanted to be as far away from Hollywood as possible. Herb Aller, who was the guild business agent, gave me a permit to shoot that film, but he said I couldn't work in this country. Then Dick Rush, who I had done some biker movies with — including the one that got me *Easy Rider* — did a picture called *Getting Straight* at Columbia Pictures. That was my first studio film. I was on the roster, but only in Group Three, which meant I could only work for Dick's company; they loaned me to Columbia Pictures for that project.

Did you and Vilmos try to form your own guild?

Kovacs: Actually, there were about 18 of us who were kind of renegades, including Vilmos, Conrad Hall, Bill Fraker, Jordan Cronenweth and Mario Tosi. We had our own little organization, and we would meet in Malibu and talk about the films we were making. They elected me president, probably because they thought I was the biggest renegade. We felt the guild was very important, but we wanted to elevate our position as cinematographers. We despised being considered technicians just because we were using cameras, lights and different equipment.

Were you technically oriented?

Kovacs: Not at all. I used a light meter. I also operated my own camera until *Five Easy Pieces* and *Alex in Wonderland.* [*Ed. Note:* Kovacs operated on *Five Easy Pieces* for all but the last few days of principal photography, which were shot in Los Angeles.] *Alex in*

Wonderland was a studio film and I was a member of the Local, so [director] Paul Mazursky told me I had to find an operator. I was angry, upset, disappointed and discouraged, you name it. All these emotions were flying around in my head. He told me I was going to have to trust somebody.

When I discovered I couldn't operate in Los Angeles for the end of the *Five Easy Pieces* shoot, I searched and searched for an operator, and finally several people recommended Bobby Byrne. He was working on a TV series, and I arranged a lunch with him at the MGM commissary. I laid it on the line. I told him I was used to operating my own camera, and I didn't want any trouble if there were times when I wanted to operate. I remember him watching me with a kind of stern look. He didn't say anything for a while. Then he asked if I just wanted him to be a dummy. I said I just wanted to handle some complicated shots. He agreed.

It was a big help having an operator on *Alex in Wonderland.* Mazursky is a brilliant director, and having Bobby there allowed me to concentrate on lighting. I trusted Bobby more as the film went on. Finally, we had to shoot a big crowd scene, and we decided we'd better use two cameras. It was kind of a montage situation, so Bobby and I didn't know what the other one was doing. The next day at dailies, we couldn't tell which was camera A and which was camera B. It was amazing. After that I trusted him completely. Bobby and I became great friends on and off the set, and we worked together until he moved up to director of photography. He has wonderful taste and a sense of drama — everything you want in a camera operator. We worked together until I shot *New York, New York,* and for that show I found another great operator in Bobby Stevens. That's what I learned after I joined the guild: every person in the crew has an important role, and each makes a creative contribution. You know, part of the *Easy Rider* crew is still working with me.

First published in *Cuts,* November 1998.

PHOTO: SUZANNE HANOVER

Vilmos Zsigmond visits Kovacs on the set of *Jack Frost* (1998), which is decorated with artificial snow.

2

Zsigmond and Kovacs: The Journey Continues

by

Bob Fisher

TRUE STORY: It was 1956. Hungary had been held captive behind the Iron Curtain since the Russian army routed the Nazis in 1945. Dissidents were parading in the streets. The Voice of America was urging them to overthrow the Communist regime with insinuations that help was on the way. Just when it seemed the government would topple, Russian troops and tanks stormed into Budapest.

Vilmos Zsigmond, ASC and Laszlo Kovacs, ASC, met on a street corner during that turmoil. It was the beginning of a lifelong friendship. Zsigmond was born and raised in Szeged, Hungary, where he worked in a factory until the commissars sent him to film school in Budapest. Kovacs was raised on a farm 60 miles outside of Budapest. Zsigmond had just graduated from the Academy of Drama and Film Art, and Kovacs was in his senior year.

"We were in different classes and didn't really know each other," Kovacs explains. "We felt we had to do something about what was happening, so we did what we knew best."

Zsigmond and Kovacs appropriated a camera from the school, and with many other cinematographers, they began recording acts of bravery and brutality as unarmed civilians tried to stop tanks. They hid the camera in a shopping bag. One served as a lookout while the other operated the camera. After the revolt was crushed, they holed up in an apartment, waiting for the storm to pass. George Illes, their mentor and head of the film school, warned them that the Communists were arresting intellectuals suspected of sympathizing with the revolt.

"The Russians blamed the revolt on spies from the West and counter-revolutionaries," Zsigmond recalls. "We wanted the world to know the truth. That meant we had to get our film out of the country."

They stuffed 30,000 feet of film into laundry bags, which they dragged through the woods in the direction of the Austrian border. About a mile from their destination, Zsigmond and Kovacs saw a Russian patrol in a village. They hid the film in a cornfield and walked into the village. While they were being questioned, Kovacs remembered he had hidden incriminating negatives in his boot. "A Russian colonel searched me," he recalls. "I'll never know if he missed the pictures, or saw them and decided to let us go. One of the villagers vouched for us; he said our families were waiting for us. That night a Hungarian border guard rowed us across the river. A lab in Vienna processed our film and made a print, but none of the TV networks was interested. They said it was old news. A producer bought our film. He gave us an old Arriflex camera and enough money to pay our lab bill."

THE JOURNEY

In March 1958, Zsigmond and Kovacs migrated separately to the United States with 30,000-40,000 other political refugees. Kovacs worked for a photographer and in a maple-syrup factory in upstate New York. Within a year he found a job processing newsreels at a lab in Seattle.

The congregation of a Lutheran church in Chicago sponsored Zsigmond. Within a year he moved to Los Angeles, where he found work in a film lab making black-and-white prints.

Kovacs soon moved to Los Angeles, where he got a job processing microfilm for a title insurance company. During their spare hours, he and Zsigmond shot 16mm educational, medical and training films. By the early 1960s they had crossed over to narrative filmmaking. The budgets were Spartan at best, and they were usually paid with promises linked to anticipated profits. "I bought a 16mm Arriflex camera and lenses and modified them for Techniscope," Zsigmond recounts. "By then, Kodak color negative and print films had improved enough for us to make blow-ups in 35mm CinemaScope. For $100 a day, you got my camera, my lights and me."

In 1963, Kovacs shot a Western over a weekend. The $12,000 budget was used to rent saddles, horses and guns. The actors and crew were building reels. The lab even processed the film and made an answer print against the promise of a deferred payment. The movie was never released, but the production manager introduced Kovacs to a young director named Richard Rush, who liked the reel.

Kovacs began shooting "motorcycle films" with titles such as *A Man Called Dagger* and *Hell's Angels on Wheels* for Rush. He was also working with other promising directors, including Peter Bogdanovich (*What's Up, Doc?, Paper Moon*), Robert Altman *(A Cold Day in the Park*) and Dennis Hopper (*Easy Rider, The Last Movie*). When Hopper asked him to shoot *Easy Rider,* Kovacs had had his fill of shooting motorcycle films — until Hopper acted out the story. They shot *Easy Rider* in 12 weeks with a single camera, a minimal lighting package and no room on the truck for a dolly. While it has the look and feel of an improvised film, Kovacs says, every scene was carefully rehearsed and staged. "We never suspected how revolutionary it was going to be or how successful it would become," Kovacs says. "I saw *Easy Rider* as an opportunity to show the world the country I had adopted."

In 1971, Kovacs introduced Zsigmond to Robert Altman, who was planning a new type of Western called *McCabe & Mrs. Miller*. Altman asked to see a sample of Zsigmond's work. "I showed him a short feature called *Prelude* [directed by John Astin]," Zsigmond says. "It was the best film I had shot at that point. Fortunately, he liked it." Zsigmond created a faded-photograph period look by pre-flashing the film to alter the contrast ratio. Where do ideas like that come from? He can only shrug in reply and point to his heart. *McCabe & Mrs. Mill*er is considered a classic, but Zsigmond points out that the actors lived in houses and teepees built as sets. They cooked their own meals and bathed in a bathhouse that was a prop. "Altman surrounded himself with great actors," Zsigmond says, "but recognition came later."

HAPPY ENDINGS

Both cinematographers have compiled extraordinary bodies of work. Zsigmond has nearly 60 credits, including *Deliverance, Cinderella Liberty, The Long Goodbye, The Rose, The Witches of Eastwick, Maverick* and *The Ghost and the Darkness.* He earned an Oscar® for *Close Encounters of the Third Kind* and other nominations for *The River* and *The Deer Hunter. The Deer Hunter* also won a British Society of Cinematographers award. He earned an Emmy® and an ASC Outstanding Achievement Award for the miniseries *Stalin.* Zsigmond is the 1999 recipient of the American Society of Cinematographers Lifetime Achievement Award, which he will receive in Los Angeles in February 2000. Kovacs has also compiled some 60 credits, including *Five Easy Pieces, The King of Marvin Gardens, Shampoo, New York, New York, The Runner Stumbles, Ghostbusters, Mask, Radio Flyer* and *My Best Friend's Wedding.* Kovacs received two Lifetime Achievement Awards for cinematography in 1998, one at CamerImage in Torun, Poland, and the other at the Hawaii International Film Festival.

THE STORY CONTINUES

Both cinematographers recently played prominent roles in bringing extraordinary films to cinema screens. For Zsigmond it was *Playing by Heart*, an independent feature developed by Hyperion Studios and released by Miramax. The film is a love story written by Willard Carroll, whose directing career is just getting underway. Carroll cast Zsigmond in the role of cinematographer because "he's shot some of my favorite films." Zsigmond says he "wanted to make a character-driven movie in 'Scope."

He adds, "It reminded me of my early days in Hollywood when I did little pictures. It tells a real story and recaptures the joy of filmmaking."

Kovacs brought *Jack Frost*, a modern-day fable featuring a 10-year-old boy and a digitally augmented snowman, to the screen. It was filmed mainly on a makeshift soundstage, where he used light to create the illusion of night and day and huge TransLites to conjure up a sense of place. It was director Troy Miller's first narrative feature; it was also filmed in widescreen. Miller was astounded when Kovacs agreed to shoot his little film about a snowman and a child. Kovacs told him, "I have a 10-year-old daughter, and I want to shoot a film she can be proud of. It's important to show your love for your children today, because sometimes tomorrow never comes."

First published in *International Film Festival,* January/February 1999.

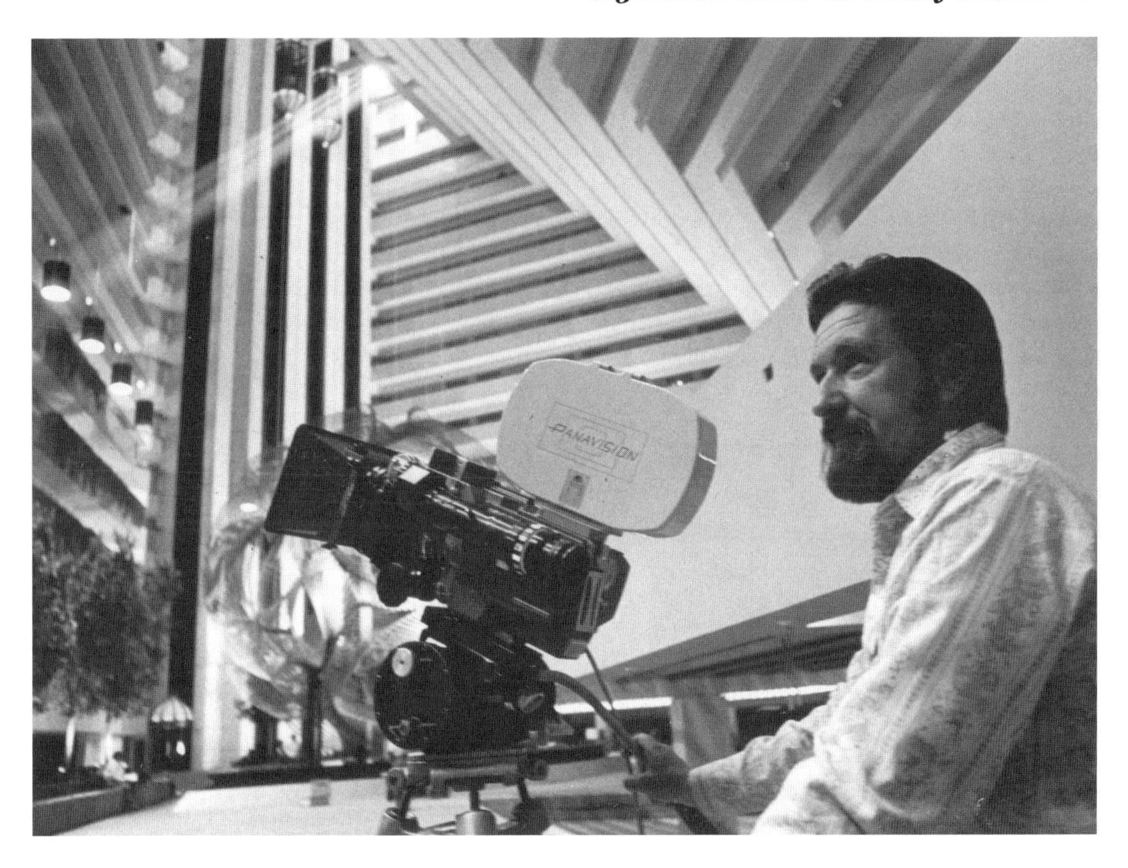

Kovacs on the set of *Freebie and the Bean* (1974) with the new, specially modified Panavision camera. Kovacs and Zsigmond competed to see who could get the camera first.

Kovacs confers with director William A. Fraker, ASC during filming of *The Legend of the Lone Ranger* (1981).

3

Behind the Cameras on *The Legend of the Lone Ranger*

The special challenges of photographing a classic Western — especially when the director himself is one of the world's top cinematographers.

by

Laszlo Kovacs, ASC

Our concept in planning the visuals for *The Legend of the Lone Ranger* was to make an old-fashioned Western. Therefore, a lot of things were done in the way we did them because Billy Fraker, the director, didn't mind admitting that he wanted a picture to pay tribute to John Ford, a Western in the old tradition. I respected him completely for this point of view.

We spent two weeks in Monument Valley (which is "John Ford country") in order to shoot the opening sequence of the picture, and it was a fabulous experience. I had been to Monument Valley before, but I had never been so close to it and I didn't realize what it meant. We walked into the valley in April, and suddenly it was like walking through John Ford's movies. You see all of those magnificent buttes and you hear the sounds of the stagecoach, the cavalry and all of that. It was a very bizarre and fantastic feeling.

We started by shooting scenes of the stagecoach arriving at the waystation. That's the first time we see the young Lone Ranger-to-be, John Reid, and the young lady who later becomes a sort of half-romantic interest for the Lone Ranger. Basically the story of the film is how he becomes the Lone Ranger, and about 80 percent of the picture dwells on that. Only in the last 20 percent of the action do you see him wearing the mask and seeking justice and becoming a true folk hero as the Lone Ranger.

In Monument Valley, we filmed the chase that develops when two bad guys suddenly take out after the stagecoach. In that sequence we duplicated a stunt that had only been done once before, by Yakima Canutt in John Ford's 1936 version of *Stagecoach*. We staged it in our version with six horses (instead of the original four). One of the bad guys (in this case, a stuntman named Terry Leonard) jumps on one of the lead horses of the team. He gets shot and falls between the horses. He is dragged all the way under the horses and the stagecoach and then is supposed to grab the end of the stagecoach and climb up on top. Leonard rehearsed the stunt many times in town before going out to the location. When we shot the stunt, he made it, except that the last horse accidentally stepped on his thigh. He lost balance and control and let go, and the right wheel went right over both of his legs. He had a lot of bruises, and we thought he had broken every bone in his body, but he was incredibly lucky.

He didn't finish the stunt the way that it was supposed to be finished, but nevertheless he finished it, so his stuntmen colleagues recognized that fact and gave him credit for doing it. The hairy thing about that stunt was the fact that it had to be filmed straight through by one camera. The stunt doesn't work if you cut it up. It has to work in one continuous shot. Otherwise it looks like it was done in pieces.

Billy Fraker maintained a very straight storyline — no camp, no making fun, no playing jokes with the content. In addition, the film was done on such a magnificent scale. Billy was constantly fighting for every single value he could put on the screen — horses, wardrobe, the Western street and the rugged locations. Being a cinematographer himself, he kept trying to help me shoot at the right time of day, if that was possible, but eventually we couldn't afford that kind of luxury, and I said, "Don't worry about it. I'll manage it."

In the film, John Reid comes to Texas to visit his older brother, who tries to get him to join the Texas Rangers. John doesn't want to join, but after the uncle of the young lady he has met on the stagecoach is ambushed in his newspaper office and killed by members of the Cavendish Gang, he joins the Rangers in an attempt to track the gang down. They arrive in Bryant's Gap, where they are ambushed by the gang. In this huge canyon, one by one the Rangers are systematically killed off. (This was an incredibly grueling sequence to shoot.) John Reid, who is not quite dead, is found by Tonto (his childhood Indian friend) and nursed back to health.

After Reid buries all the Rangers, we see him from behind; then he gets up, turns around, and for the first time we see him with the mask on. He puts on his hat, gets on the horse and rides away. He is now the Lone Ranger, and that's the first time we hear Rossini's *William Tell* Overture. It's played very straight.

Up to this point, the story has been treated visually in a very muted, very subdued manner: earth-colored, brown-textured, sepia, lots of dust (incredible amounts of Fullers earth were used in every shot). It was a downright dirty Western environment that we created, because that was what Billy Fraker wanted. He wanted truth in the look of the images, the behavior of the characters, the dramatics of the action, the wardrobe, the set dressing, everything.

But then, when John Reid became the Lone Ranger, we changed colors. The picture became red, white and blue — the great American story. No more subdued colors. It was a big change. An American legend came alive, and from that point on we tried to impose primary colors — literally red, white and blue — not to duplicate the American flag, but in order to achieve the brightness of the old Technicolor look, which is hard to get without the three-strip process.

In the last part of the picture, Cavendish kidnaps President Grant, and the Lone Ranger and Tonto sneak into the gang's compound at night to free him. They plant dynamite everywhere, and the next morning they start blowing up the place. Then the cavalry comes riding to rescue the president, with the two horses, Silver and Scout, charging full-out through the water, leading the whole pack of 150 cavalrymen. It was an incredible sight. I've never seen anything like it. I don't know how the animal trainers did it, but it gave me goosebumps.

Much of the action takes place in Del Rio, a town in southwest Texas, which was actually an enormous set built especially for this picture outside of Santa Fe. It's probably the largest existing Western set in the country at this time. The west end of the town is Mexican and the east end is Anglo. At one end of the main street is a Mexican adobe church, and at the other end is a three-story courthouse. There are also a newspaper office, opera house, Wells Fargo office, hotels, saloons, a cantina and a lot of Mexican adobe buildings.

What is admirable is that the construction crew built the "town" from scratch in just seven weeks. I think it cost about $1 million, and they just left it there. It's right across from the state prison on flat land, from which you can look in almost any direction without seeing any structures. The town was laid out so that one end of the main street faced the sunrise and the other end faced the sunset. The only problem was that the production selected the site in February, and we were shooting in June, during which time the sun shifted! Nevertheless, we used that layout to good advantage, and that's what gave me the control I needed.

Most of the time I could shoot with backlight and arrange my own little schedule with the production manager. We would start in the morning, shooting certain scenes with backlight, and in the afternoon we would get reverse coverage and shoot into backlight again. I really believe that you can get away with this, and I've been doing it for years. If you look at the film, you'll see that most of the cuts within a sequence are backlit, no matter in which direction the camera is pointed.

Theoretically, the reverse of a backlit scene should be in frontlight, but I can't deal with that kind of reality. I can't stand it because it's awful. But if the shifting around in backlight is done correctly, the audience will never be aware of it — and they shouldn't be. As a matter of fact, if you see one backlit scene cut after another in an opposite reverse, they tend to blend together for the eye. I'm never going to question that. But if, after the backlit shot, I cut to a reverse shot that's frontlit, to me it's terribly bothersome, even though it's real. This kind of reality can change a bit with the help of a director who will say, "I don't care. Just tell me which way you want to shoot." That's why it's a pleasure to work with a cinematographer/director like Bill Fraker.

On the Del Rio set, we had a night sequence in which there was an All Saints Day procession. The Rangers are at the cantina, and John Reid meets the young lady again after the stagecoach ride. To film the sequence, we shot for two full weeks, every night, all night, and sometimes it would rain. We got snowed in in the middle of May! We got four inches of snow and we still had to shoot. It got slushy at the end of the day, and at night we froze. It was the most brutal kind of cold. Nobody in the crew had expected it to be so cold, so we didn't have warm-enough clothes. On top of that, we had to shoot a love scene under the arches of the cantina. It wasn't very much fun for the actors, either!

The night sequence was absolutely enormous because Billy wanted to see the depth of the entire town. The first shot starts from above the church, with all of the piñatas exploding. That's a transition shot from the execution. The screen is totally white after the piñatas explode, and as the smoke clears you see a long, long Western street, with the crowd of Mexican women and children carrying religious objects and singing, and the stalls selling all kinds of goodies.

Filming this sequence presented an enormous lighting problem. We had to order 80 or 90 extra 10Ks, an extra rigging crew of five and all kinds of extra units and generators, and I had to have the whole town electrically serviced. We had a rigging crew there for two weeks before we arrived, and my gaffer and I had to coordinate the rigging crew; no matter what part of the town we would be shooting, or which direction, I wanted service to be right there.

We had to put the cables underground, and they had to be designed to handle any amount of load in any section of the town. Billy had the set designed so that the width of the main street was exaggerated; it was probably twice as wide as it normally would be. He separated the buildings so that in any direction you might shoot, you'd always see some open space. You see the depth, you see the flat country, and you see Texas. It was not a clustered Western town, with the buildings built right on top of each other. The space was utilized beautifully, but this very spread-out characteristic also presented a problem for me, especially for night shooting.

I had to reach from one side of the street to a building on the opposite side that was frontlit with a gaslight or lantern effect. In addition, there was enormous action in the streets that sometimes involved a lot of stunts. There were little dialogue scenes between two or three people, but you saw the whole world. Even close up, you could see a mile. This added up to a tremendous physical and electrical problem. We had to bring in the biggest generators from Hollywood, Houston and Chicago because we were burning really heavy loads.

For this sequence, I wanted a special bronze kind of look, but not quite sepia, because it's hard to get sepia. I was interested in getting a monochrome warm tone, which was completely justified by the fact that all of the light sources were candles, lanterns or oil lamps — all very warm sources. Whether inside or outside, the presence of these warm sources justified my shifting even further to the amber side. I used either light straw or light amber gels on every single unit except the fill light; the fill was the only white light.

To further enhance the warm effect, I talked to Skip Nicholson at Technicolor about adding even more warmth in the printing, and that helped it. We finally arrived at a printing light, and the effect tied in with the subdued look of the first part of the picture, which changed only after John Reid became the Lone Ranger — after that, the colors grew as alive and bright as the *William Tell* Overture.

The shoot was a really hard experience, because if you try to do a Western authentically, there are so many elements to cope with that create physical and logistical problems. The horses alone are a major problem. In the picture you see the two horses, Silver and Scout, but we actually had six Silvers and two Scouts. Silver, especially, had to do some "acting." So one Silver was the close-up horse, because his face was the most beautiful. There was another Silver who could rear beautifully. Another could ride like hell, "fast as a silver bullet." Another could back up, all on voice command. Each horse had its own specialty; put them all together and you had Silver. Scout was a low-key, smart little pinto. We had two identical, beautiful horses for Scout, in case one of them was overworked or got sick or whatever.

On top of that, we had 150 cavalry. They were all local people who could ride well, but strict attention had to be paid to their wardrobe, their hair, their makeup, their weapons; everything had to be totally correct.

The Cavendish stronghold was built at the bottom of a canyon, which we flooded with about a foot of water. There was a flume across the waterway, and we dammed it up out of sight to wind past the curve of the canyon. We had a little spring coming through and feeding the waterway. One day the spring went dry and we had to bring the water in, 30,000 gallons of water in trucks. They had to cut roads for the trucks. The reason was that Billy Fraker wanted that special look for the climactic sequence when the cavalry rescues President Grant.

This was a big battle sequence. At the main gate of the Cavendish Gang stronghold was a wall built of logs the size of telephone poles, like the wall in *King Kong*. When the gates in that wall are blown up, there is knee-deep water and you see Silver and Scout riding at you full-blast. Behind them are the generals and 150 cavalrymen riding full-out, as the two horses take them right into the compound. The Lone Ranger jumps on Silver and chases Cavendish, and there's a huge fight between the Cavendish people and the cavalry. It's magnificent stuff as they come running through the water.

Naturally, there was always dust — we called it "texture." ("We need more texture!") In every shot, the special-effects people had to deal with explosions, smoke or dust, or all three. The feeling that these elements create on screen is magnificent; it looks terrific, but it's miserable to work with. It gets into your lungs. Even in Santa Fe, which probably has the cleanest air in the world, you feel like you are back in Los Angeles, smelling and eating the smog, because your lungs never clear up. In the interior sets, in a bar or cantina, there are always smoky candles or oil lamps burning on tables. Smoke is always very prominent, and I don't think you question it. You expect it. If it's not there, you ask, "What happened?"

For other sequences, we were able to use the most magnificent part of New Mexico. I'm a great New Mexico fan; I just love that country so much, and I've done several pictures there — the major part of *Butch and Sundance,* part of *Easy Rider*, and a sequence for *Pocket Money*. It has some of the most fabulous natural beauty in the world, plus a ruggedness that provides hardship to work against. The whole place is such a beautiful natural phenomenon. Each wash or canyon is probably seven million years old, carved out of the sandstone by wind or water. The walls of a canyon may go up a sheer 60 or 80 feet, but the bottom of it is so narrow that two horses can barely pass each other. Sometimes just one horse can go by.

It is in a canyon like that that the Rangers are ambushed by the Cavendish Gang. They dynamite the rock at each end of the canyon so the Rangers can't get out, and then they open fire from above. Such locations are very important dramatically. They have to be believable and fearsome and, at the same time, have enormous beauty, like the area in New Mexico called Tent Rocks, in which each rock formation looks like a teepee.

The advantage of working out of Santa Fe is that within an hour's drive of the city you can reach any type of terrain. For example, just 18 miles from the center of town, across from the prison where they had the horrendous riot this year, there is a huge, incredible plateau on which we built our version of Del Rio. Up in the higher country are all kinds of meadows and mountain lakes, and the natural beauty never ends. Working against this kind of background provided me with a great deal of consolation and happiness.

One may think of *The Legend of the Lone Ranger* as basically an exterior picture, and that's true, but we had some interiors that were important to the story. Then there was the special challenge of working at night on a vast scale. Supposedly, during night shooting you have "total control," because you can see what you light and how you light. When you're shooting daytime exteriors you are really at the mercy of the "Big Gaffer in the Sky." This picture provided a terrific balance between day and night shooting, so I didn't get bored with the exterior stuff. When you are able to light, you become more excited.

In dealing with this kind of subject matter, there are enormous numbers of extras and horses and good guys and bad guys, so you end up using multiple cameras. During the entire production I had two camera crews, and for the big sequences I had four and sometimes five. This added up to a very large camera crew. I think I had 11 or 12 people, including assistants and operators. For this kind of action it's important to have talented operators, because many times you are unable to tell them exactly what is going to happen and what to go for. I like to see them use their own initiative and make their own decisions, especially on stunts. Very often you can't count on a stunt happening the way it was planned; you have to expect the unexpected. The operators have to be very alert. I was lucky. I had some beautiful guys who did a beautiful job.

Dealing with all of the problems and coordinating with everybody to make sure each person is doing the right thing is a very big responsibility, but you have a much better chance of coping with it if you have enough preproduction time to talk with the director, to really get close to his problems, to find out how he feels about the look and the style of the photography. Those are the moments that are very crucial to the making of a film.

I had some prep time on this picture, but not much, unfortunately. Four days before I started *The Lone Ranger* I was [still] working on *Inside Moves*. Bill Fraker and I would get together on weekends and do a lot of talking about the project. I had a chance to select some of the locations, and I suggested a few places that I knew from previous experience. But Billy had to do most of the scouting with the production designer, Al Brenner, and I must say that they did a beautiful job. I couldn't have been happier when I learned what the locations were going to be.

On the first day of shooting, all the talking you've done becomes academic — you put it in a bag, seal it up and somebody throws it away. It's like it never happened, but all of it is right there in your head. And it had better be in your hands as well, because the director cannot deal with it anymore. He has other problems, and there is not another word said about it again. But when the dailies are screened, it had better be there! Otherwise you're through, no matter who you're working with.

The interiors on this picture were basically small and not very elaborate. There was the Mexican cantina, which the Rangers frequented and where we shot several sequences. There were some church interiors, which were actually shot in existing churches around Santa Fe. We had a warehouse in which the construction people put together prefabricated set elements. They also built a couple of interiors of the Cavendish stronghold, a huge dining room and the bedroom where President Grant was held captive. The interiors were not an especially challenging factor, but as I've said before, the night exteriors were. I was using 18 electricians and 18 grips, more than I've ever had on any other picture, but at times I felt that I could have used more because the lighting was so spread out. We had to communicate with walkie-talkies, and we had huge towers on which two, three or four 1OKs were rigged.

The grips had prepared some teasers in case they had to use gobo lights from certain areas or shield the lenses. I didn't realize what a huge job it was until we started doing it. You prepare for every possible situation, but basically the problems all arrive when you walk onto the set and the sun is getting lower and lower, and it's getting darker and darker, and the director walks over to you and says, "Call me when you're ready." At about 10 p.m., the assistant director walks over to you and says, "Are you ready yet?" No way, not even halfway through.

We had, of course, talked about all this very realistically. The production people realized that if we got one shot that night, we would be very lucky. What happened was that at about 4 a.m., I was ready for the big master shot. They had about 500 extras fully dressed, shivering cold, waiting, and I felt that I had to do something. But it wasn't just that; I wouldn't have done it if I'd felt that I had to make a tremendous compromise.

Of course, everything is something of a compromise when you are making movies. You start with 100 percent in your mind, and you're lucky if you end up getting 70 percent. You're terrific if you get 80 percent. But you have to draw the line either way, decide not to go any lower or reach any higher. You have to know what your budgetary and production limits are, which is another part of making films. It's the ugly part, but you have to deal with it. I feel that I was able to hit about 80 percent on *The Lone Ranger*. I was lucky.

In the case of shooting the big fiesta sequence at night, I tried to light every area that might possibly be used for action, but not waste my time lighting something that would never get onto film. At times I would say to Billy, "Could you bring your actors and just give me another rehearsal?" Maybe there is another change you'd like to make in blocking or staging. I don't want to be locked into something and have to say, "I can't do this. I didn't plan on this." Billy was very understanding, and it really worked to the advantage of the film. Either he or I would have an idea that we wanted to incorporate, and then he would walk away and I would work on it.

That night we were able to get the master shot with four cameras, a big vista that established the entire sequence. It worked very well and really carried through in terms of the visual design that Billy and Al Brenner had laid out for the space. There was a kind of visual unity to it.

I used no Brute arcs in lighting the fiesta sequence, the reason being that Brutes tie down too many men. You just can't afford it. I would have needed 20 more electricians, and it just wasn't practical. I used arcs, very heavily diffused through various materials, on the day sequences. Unfortunately, HMI units did not have the intensity or throw that I needed for my day exteriors. They are great lights, but when you're outdoors and have to reach a certain distance (to photograph two horsemen talking, for example), they don't reach far enough to provide adequate fill light. Where the HMIs really come in handy is in more or less confined interiors; they give you a beautiful color balance, and there is enough intensity that you can bounce them. You can either make them soft or use them as hard light. They are very flexible in a situation like that. But for straight daylight exteriors I had to use the Brutes.

On the Bryant's Gap sequence, where the Cavendish Gang ambushes the Texas Rangers, we had scenes playing up on top of the canyon, as well as down in the bowels of it.

It was actually like three huge layers of action, each at a different level, but covering a vast expanse. I knew that I couldn't do it with reflectors; they're terrible. Billy also wanted to do a big dolly shot there, so we picked the actual spot days before and hired a helicopter to hoist all the lumber up there to build the tracks over the rocky terrain, and also to lift a very heavy dolly. (A lighter dolly wouldn't hold up on a Western.) So as long as they were ferrying all that equipment up there, I said, "Let's take two Brutes up there, too." It was very difficult to maneuver on top, but those two Brutes did the job just perfectly. Brutes are wonderful things in such a situation. Every type of light has its own place, and you have to select the right type of light to suit a particular situation.

As far as camera movement was concerned, Billy Fraker's idea was to not make so many camera moves that the picture would take on a contemporary look. He preferred the philosophy of John Ford, who used to say, "Don't move the camera; move the people." So he tended to move the people within the composition, bringing them forward and moving them out. So we did have some camera moves, but I would say that in general, when we couldn't find any other way to do it, we would do it with the dolly.

Using the crane was a different story — you can't make a Western without a crane. We had one huge tracking shot in the night sequence. The actors start at the church and move up, walking and talking all the way back. For that we had to use the Chapman Titan crane with an offset arm, because we didn't want a 45-degree angle. We wanted it much straighter. If you try to do a straight-on pullback with a dolly or a conventional crane, you see the tracks behind the actors or right next to them, especially in the anamorphic format. That particular shot worked out very well, but our basic concept was not to move the camera.

Working on *The Legend of the Lone Ranger* was an exciting experience, and I'm really glad that I was able to get involved in doing a true Western. Such a story lives in people's minds as a folk tale, because the characters are not real. Throughout the '30s, '40s and '50s, the myth of the Lone Ranger became so strong in people's minds that they believed the characters really existed in the Old West. That's what we tried to convey in making the film, the real story that everybody is familiar with — how he became the Lone Ranger and a legend.

First published in *American Cinematographer*, July 1981.

Kovacs (far right) films a 1930s movie-in-the-making for a scene in *Frances* (1982).

Cinematography for *Frances*

by

Richard Patterson

When you have three very strong, creative people, you have to make sure that all three people are working on the same picture and not on three different pictures. It can happen, you know, but this was a very exciting experience for me because we were able to channel our thinking very closely and find a common denominator for everything."

Laszlo Kovacs is describing his collaboration with director Graeme Clifford and production designer Richard Sylbert on *Frances*. The common denominator was a shared sense of the meaning of the film, a sense of the overall emotional impact the film was supposed to have. It was a sense of something intangible that could not be summed up in words, but which nonetheless influenced every choice in the making of the film. Kovacs' job as director of photography was largely a matter of developing this sense of the film during preproduction so that he could translate it into lights, lenses, filters and framing during the production.

Frances is the life story of Frances Farmer, an actress who appeared in 14 films from 1936 to 1942, most notably *Come and Get It*. It is a story of extremes, of her rise to stardom and her descent into an incredible abyss of prisons and mental institutions. It is a portrait of a fiercely independent woman, an idealist and a maverick who was at odds with the Establishment, her mother and, ultimately, herself. On one level it's the story of a conflict between society and the individual in which society wins, an indictment of Farmer's mother, the psychiatric profession and the studio executives who conspired to break her spirit, even to the point of operating on her brain. On another level it's the story of a bright and beautiful woman who, for a variety of complex reasons, embarks on a journey of self-destruction.

Frances was Clifford's first film as a director. He was the editor on Bob Rafelson's version of *The Postman Always Rings Twice* and several other films, including *F.I.S.T.*, which Kovacs shot for Norman Jewison. Clifford and Kovacs first met in 1968, when

Kovacs shot *A Cold Day in the Park* and Clifford was working as an assistant director to Robert Altman. When Clifford called Kovacs to ask him if he were interested in shooting *Frances*, Kovacs' first reaction was, "Frances who?" He knew nothing about Farmer; but when Clifford described the story to him briefly, Kovacs immediately felt that he had to work on the film. For one thing, the story spans the Thirties, Forties and Fifties; Kovacs had worked with the latter period on *F.I.S.T.* and describes it as his absolute favorite period. More importantly, however, he responded very strongly to the storyline Clifford described.

Clifford sent Kovacs a copy of the script, which was still undergoing revisions, and then suggested that Kovacs read *Shadowland*, William Arnold's biography of Farmer. Kovacs read both and then spent as much time as possible during the five or six months of preproduction trying to absorb the research about Farmer that had already been done by Clifford, production designer Sylbert and producers Marie Yates and Jonathan Sanger. He says it is essential for a director of photography to understand all the elements in a picture. "It's not enough to just be a cinematographer or photographer. You can't just light a set and shoot the scene; you have to understand emotionally what the character is going through. You have to understand the scene, the dramatic structure, the relationships, and the character motivations — all the whys. You have to know the answers to those whys."

This is, of course, especially true of a character piece like *Frances*, which Kovacs describes as a "one-person show, a tour de force [by Jessica Lange, who portrays Farmer]." The first stage in the process for Kovacs is to absorb as much information, to take in as many impressions as he can, until an intuitive sense begins to develop inside him. It may sound simple, but it does not come easily, he notes. "You have to collect a lot of information about the subject, learn more and more about the character and the period, the political and economic problems of the time. You can't understand Frances Farmer without understanding the labor movement of the Thirties, the theater [scene] in New York and Hollywood. It's very complex. Frances was a multi-layered person."

Kovacs had innumerable conversations with Clifford and Sylbert, and they screened all of Farmer's films, but the real inspiration for him came when he was able to see locations or sets. Sylbert had done a great deal of work before Kovacs came on board, and the cinematographer recalls a location scouting trip to Seattle, where Sylbert conducted a walking tour of Farmer's old neighborhood, including her house, the high school, the beach and a bar where she used to hang out. They also visited a mental hospital where Farmer spent several years, even though they knew they could never get permission to film there. All the while Clifford, was explaining how he viewed the story and what he wanted from the various elements. "And I soaked this information up," says Kovacs, "just looking, watching and asking questions or listening to all the discussions."

Eventually Kovacs began to develop a sense of the film's tone and texture. After he has absorbed enough information and become sufficiently attuned to the director's vision, "I begin to feel it," he says. "And it's a feeling which has two meanings: you not only feel it emotionally, but you also sense it. You can almost put your finger on it. You can't describe it precisely, but you can begin to talk about textures and color tones and compositional elements. You can say it's about harshness, for example. You know what calls for symmetry or movement."

Kovacs feels particularly fortunate to have worked with Sylbert, whom he says is a production designer in the true sense of the word. "His choices are so defined and precise, so exact in terms of the framework of what the director wants to do. He basically materializes everything that has been discussed."

While he emphasizes that it is the director who interprets the drama and sets the pace, Kovacs does not hesitate to give a large share of the credit for the visual design of *Frances* to the production designer. It seems fairly clear that much of the film's impact is due to the very deliberate and detailed design work by Sylbert, and that what Kovacs was able to do was build on that work and refine it by means of a lighting and camera style that was in harmony with it. He and Sylbert had detailed discussions about the composition of images for various scenes, and Kovacs even says that many of Sylbert's sets seemed to be designed so that there was only one right way to shoot them. Kovacs was delighted to have them that way, because he always understood what Sylbert was trying to achieve with a set and felt that it was right for the picture.

Kovacs viewed the production design from several different perspectives. The most obvious aspects are, of course, the period considerations; the sets, costumes and props had to be appropriate for the period. Kovacs cites Sylbert's familiarity with New York and the whole world of the theater as a boon for the production, but he notes that historical accuracy is not what Sylbert is really about; rather, it's only a foundation on which he builds the rest of the design.

Frances is a classic example of the orchestration of graphic elements in the design of a movie. Color, texture and composition are very carefully chosen to give the film a graphic structure that reinforces its dramatic or narrative structure. After viewing the picture, one need only look at stills from it to recall how the design of the film does, in fact, contribute to the orchestration of a viewer's emotions. The nature of Farmer's home; the contrasts between that home and Hollywood or New York; the relationship between home, Hollywood and the mental institution; and the resolution of the conflicts are all sensed through color and texture as well as dialogue and action. As Kovacs puts in when discussing the different ways he lit and photographed the set for the Farmer house, "Every time you go back to that house, it is different; something is different. Either relationships have changed, or there are strangers in the house, or whatever, and those qualities had to be translated into lighting to instantly be put on the screen. As soon as the audience sees the first frame, they should understand the feeling, what's going on there, before any actors open their mouths. That's the power of cinema — if it's right, you can tell more with one frame than with a page of dialogue."

Another aspect of Sylbert's production design is the way in which the sets comment on the characters. The most striking examples of this are scenes involving the playwright Clifford Odets. Kovacs describes his reaction on first seeing the set for Odets' New York apartment: "The set was being built on a stage next to where we were working, and I was tempted to stick my head in and take a peek, but I said, 'No, I don't want to look at it. I just want to go with it. I'll look at it when it's fully dressed.' Sylbert was working very closely with the set decorator, George Gaines, who has a wonderful sense of detail. If he knows you as a character, he knows exactly what kind of pen you would use! So I decided to wait until the set was finished, and when I finally walked into the completed set, I said, 'My God, *that's* the way he was? This guy can't be that egotistical or narcissistic.' The set really reflects the personality of the character, and I understood exactly what Sylbert was trying to convey. I felt like saying to him, 'This is fantastic. You make my job so easy because what you present is so clear-cut conceptually that anybody with a brain can understand the intent.'"

One of the ways Sylbert created that impression in Odets' apartment was by the use of white. The white of the apartment not only connects it thematically with the setting in Hollywood, but also contributes to the sense of elegance that contrasts so sharply with the drab intensity of the sets for the theater where Odets' play is being produced. It is as though the two environments in which we see Odets capture perfectly two sides of his personality: the idealistic playwright and the self-centered lover.

What Kovacs did, then, in shooting scenes in Odets' apartment was to make sure that there was always white in the frame. "Even if it was a big close-up of Odets," he says, "I accentuated his big, puffy white shirtsleeve. Or when Frances is told by the theater manager that she can't go to London with the play, she stands up, and there is a white bookcase and the white hall behind her, and she's in a dark dress with a black belt. There are no reds, blues, yellows or pinks, no other colors. Even the flower that was used in a scene in Odets' apartment was a white lily."

In addition to the color scheme, the choice of furniture and props contributed to this sense of Odets' personality, and Kovacs can recall instances when Sylbert came to him during the shoot and asked him not to include something in a shot because he realized not that it was inappropriate for the period, but that it was wrong for the character.

Another striking instance of the way in which a set comments on a character is the office that Farmer's father uses. Kovacs notes, "It's a bizarre place to have an office. Dick was looking for grandeur to contrast with the father's condition, not to belittle him, but to show that he just barely functions as a lawyer for derelicts and drunks and the poor. Your first idea of his office would probably be a little cubbyhole somewhere. You'd go for the obvious: dirty walls, dirty windows, one little desk, no pictures on the wall, nothing to look at. Instead, Dick chose a balcony in a hotel that was once very opulent. It has marble columns and stained glass, but it's run-down now, and his desk is on the mezzanine in a corner next to a pay phone. It's a place where derelicts just hang out, sitting around on the couches and chairs and waiting."

According to Kovacs, there was nothing in the script to indicate that the office was in such a place, and the design had no basis in fact. It was Sylbert's way of underscoring the father's condition. "That was Dick's intuition, and it inspired me as a cinematographer. But you have to accept the idea; you have to understand what the designer is after. And you have to realize that sometimes in filmmaking, the shortest way from A to B is not a straight line. It's very difficult to describe how you know when to take the most direct path, and when to take a detour in order to make a point visually."

Another set that Kovacs singles out as particularly effective is the black bathroom in the house where Farmer attends a party after a hard day at the studio. "Frances asks the hostess if she can use the bathroom, and the next thing we cut to is a fishbowl, and then we discover that Frances is taking a bath. Then we cut back to see that beautifully designed and totally symmetrical bathroom, with the bathtub in the middle. It gives you a kind of stable feeling, a sense that Frances is very sure of what she's doing. She has no problems at that moment, so we support that feeling with the composition. And that's how Dick Sylbert built the set; I couldn't shoot it any other way. It's just great. Dick eliminates a lot of guesswork and discussions that lead nowhere. He says, 'This is it, fellas.' And that's how we shoot it."

Kovacs says his own contribution to a film really begins during preproduction, when he is ready to shoot tests. On *Frances* there came a point when he felt he had grasped Clifford and Sylbert's ideas well enough to translate them into lighting and camera styles. He essentially said, "Okay, I understand. Now let me show you what it's going to look like on film." Kovacs shot eight days of tests, which consisted primarily of close-ups of Jessica Lange. Because of the changes that Farmer goes through in the film, it was essential to establish makeup and hair styles for the various periods in her life, and Kovacs established a lighting style to go with each look. They shot stills as well as film tests, but it was the film tests that proved the most successful. Frames were cut from the workprint and 8"x10" prints were made; the prints were put on a big board for the purpose of analyzing the structure of the film, and copies of the prints were used by the makeup artist and hairstylist during the production.

One of the things that Kovacs did not fully realize until he saw the finished film was the extent to which the whole story is encapsulated in close-ups of Farmer — not only through the changes in her face and the progression in Lange's performance, but also through the color tones and textures of the image, and the mood created by the lighting. The most obvious example of this is, of course, the contrast between the glamour lighting of the Hollywood period and the lighting for the period when Farmer was in the mental institution. For what he views as the "Golden Age of Hollywood," Kovacs literally used gold tones in the lighting, and he also used the lighting conventions of that period, namely a soft look with hard backlight. The Hollywood period was the only one for which he used backlight, except in instances where it was necessitated by a source in the scene.

For Farmer's high-school days, Kovacs used soft lights, which combined with the look of virtually no make-up to create a very soft, barren effect. He says it was a great deal easier to make Lange appear younger than she is than it was to make her appear older, and he cites the look for the late "This Is Your Life" period of Farmer's life as the one that was the most difficult to achieve. How to accomplish it was not even resolved before the film went into production, and a great deal of experimenting was done with makeup, none of which produced satisfactory results.
In the end, Kovacs decided that the key was the lighting. One thing of which he was acutely aware during the shoot was Lange's eyes. Kovacs feels that an actor's eyes are always the key to the audience's involvement in the drama, and he felt that the way in which Lange's eyes always seemed to be on the brink of watering contributed greatly to a viewer's sense of the pent-up emotion she was portraying. Thinking about his efforts to always have some light in Lange's eyes gave him the idea of shooting the final sequence without any eyelight. The result was a perfect complement to the way in which Lange portrays a woman who has undergone a lobotomy; her eyes seem lifeless in comparison to everything we have seen before. In order to achieve this effect in a sequence that involved a long dolly shot — Farmer walking and talking with an old friend (Sam Shepard) — Kovacs lit the scene from above. This created slight shadows under Lange's eyes and emphasized her cheekbones, which convincingly aged her when combined with a certain amount of make-up.

Kovacs used a Venetian blind motif to light sequences during which Farmer is committed to the mental institution. He jokes about his fondness for Venetian blind shadows as a means of conveying a sense of imprisonment, recalling that he made a great deal of use of them in *Heartbeat.* (As he puts it, he keeps waiting for someone to "nail" him for it.) Nonetheless, he felt they were effective in *Frances.* They are used first in a scene where Farmer is interviewed by the doctor of a convalescent home. The shadows do not actually hit her face in that scene, but later on, when she is committed to a state hospital, the shadows from the blinds cut across her face.

In general, Kovacs says, his lighting for *Frances* represents a transitional period; he was disciplining himself to take a much simpler approach to lighting. He says, "Lighting can be a very harrowing experience if you don't keep it simple. Now, after so many years in the business, I realize that the simpler it is, the more effective it is. I used to use so many lights, and now my approach is to use as few lights as possible to create the same effect. To me, it's more realistic and so much more believable if you keep it simple. I lit the courtroom scene where Frances is sentenced to 180 days [in jail] with about three lights. It was an actual court on the sixth or seventh floor in San Pedro, so I couldn't light through the windows."

Kovacs also prefers to use enough light to enable him to shoot at T4 in interiors. "I don't like low light levels because I think it hurts the pictorial quality. You have to use fast lenses and shallow depth of field, and it bothers me if an actor's nose is sharp and his ear is out of focus. I can't stand that. I don't know what kind of cause it can possibly serve."

Just as Sylbert designed the color scheme of the sets to reinforce the film's dramatic structure, Kovacs controlled color in the photography by using gels on the lights while shooting and by careful timing of the negative in printing. He also used color to comment on characters, as in the final scene in the Farmer house between Frances' parents. "I went back to the golden tones of the past," he says. "As the mother grows older she still has this crazy dream [about her daughter's stardom], and I don't know why, but my instinct said I should make the place look warm — like what it could have been, but isn't."

The production of *Frances* was a relatively long (four and a half months) and intense experience. Says Kovacs, "It was very emotionally taxing, because you could never divorce yourself from the intensity of Jessica's performance. You were there and you were part of it, and it just drained your emotions. Can you imagine what it did to her when she had to do it over and over?"

Kovacs estimates that the filmmakers shot about 20 percent more material than was used in the finished film, a figure that he says is normal. He adds that the script was still being revised during the production. There were some 96 sets or locations for the film, and the most difficult part of the shoot was getting everything that was needed sent to Seattle in the amount of time available. Kovacs says he likes to get involved in the scheduling of a production in order to ensure that as much time as possible is allotted for location work, which is subject to variations in weather and light.

As important as Kovacs feels it is for the cinematographer to be involved in the preproduction planning, he insists that there is a limit to how much homework a cameraman or director can do as far as the actual staging and shooting of a film is concerned — especially on a film which is so dependent upon the performances of the actors. Kovacs feels there are a lot of choices that a cinematographer makes instinctively on the set when the time comes to shoot. "I never like to go home and do my homework. Say, for instance, we are going to shoot a new scene tomorrow morning. I know the whole story of the script and the relationship of that scene to the overall structure. I also have a general idea of an approach for the lighting, but I'm not going to sit down and start working on a floorplan because it would be totally insane. The next morning I would go to the set, the director would bring in the actress and say, 'Okay, let's run through the scene,' and right there my plan would go out the window. My point is, how can anyone do a floorplan or even a mental storyboard? The only person who can really storyboard is the director, and directors are very cautious about it. When you go home and sit down in a chair, it's just you and a piece of paper; you exclude the actor, and you can't do that because actors can bring tremendous color, tremendous detail that you can never even dream of at your desk.

"Just as a face can have a thousand different moods and expressions, you can light a close-up in as many different ways. Lighting choices are choices you make on the spot when you see a scene. The importance of a good rehearsal is not just that you see the physical blocking and staging, but that you see where the emotional peaks are in the scene. You feel what the scene is about so you know what you have to support. That's when you can make decisions about lighting.

"Usually you light the wide shot first, but that doesn't have as much importance today as it did in the old days," he adds. "Many directors now use the so-called master shots to let the actors find out which direction they're going to take the scene, and many times they just throw it away. It's a good lead-in dramatically for all the creative people involved. You create the overall mood and establish the sources for the lights. Once you start playing the scene closer, you might create an additional off-camera light source. You can take poetic license in order to create an effect."

One prime example of on-the-spot, creative decision-making in *Frances* is the shot in which Farmer tells off a director on the set and exits, screaming, from the soundstage. As she throws open the door, light comes streaming in around her to create an image that seems to be a perfect correlative for her state of mind. Not only was this image not conceived beforehand, but it was born partially out of necessity because the scene was shot at night. Kovacs assured Clifford that it would be possible to create a realistic sense of a day exterior beyond the door with some greens and enough light bouncing off white muslin. Clifford agreed to shoot it that way, but Kovacs could tell that he was not totally satisfied. Then Clifford came back to ask Kovacs what he thought of the idea of completely blowing out the door so that there was nothing visible beyond it but the light pouring through the doorway. Kovacs seized upon the idea, pumped a lot more light onto the white muslin and used a fog filter on the lens to accentuate the effect.

Kovacs shot two other pictures during the time between when he finished shooting *Frances* and when he saw the finished version of it. He says he never fails to be surprised by the way a picture looks after it has been edited, and he thinks a cameraman who has been away from a picture for quite a while can bring a fresh eye to the editing process at a point when the director and editor have been working with it for months. One of the things that struck him about the editing for *Frances*, aside from the inevitable cuts made to shorten the film, was the way in which scenes from the violent ward in the hospital were intercut with Farmer's hearing before the panel to determine whether she could be released. The images that play so effectively as memories passing through Frances' mind as she confronts the panel were originally filmed as separate scenes. Changes continued to be made in the editing after Kovacs returned to supervise the timing of the answer print.

In its completed form, *Frances* is a prime example of a film in which the contributions of its various creators mesh into a cohesive whole. Each artist and craftsman has endeavored to complement the efforts of his co-workers, and the result shows on the screen.

First published in *American Cinematographer*, March 1983.

Preparing to film the massive set for the climax of *Ghostbusters* (1984).

5

Laszlo Kovacs, ASC and Ghostbusters

by

Randy Lofficier

Ghostbusters had its beginnings in the fertile mind of comedian/ writer Dan Aykroyd. One of the original stars of NBC's *Saturday Night Live*, Aykroyd's film career includes *1941* (1979), *The Blues Brothers* (1980) and *Trading Places* (1983). Aykroyd reportedly wrote a first-draft screenplay of *Ghostbusters* and showed it to longtime friend and fellow *SNL* alumnus Bill Murray. Murray and Aykroyd, in turn, took the idea to director Ivan Reitman, who was instrumental in shifting the emphasis from pure fantasy to wilder comedy.

The story, as developed, concerns a trio of Columbia University scientists — the womanizing Venkman (Murray), the money-hungry Stantz (Aykroyd) and the maniacal Spengler (Harold Ramis) — who are expelled from academia and set out to open their own business, hunting ghosts in New York City. The script includes a plethora of special effects, such as representations of various ghosts and demons, the sophisticated weaponry used by the Ghostbusters, and a climactic battle with an extra-dimensional demon named Gozer, who turns into a 112 ½'-tall marshmallow man!

Director of photography Laszlo Kovacs, ASC was chosen to photograph the picture. Kovacs' credits include *Easy Rider; The King of Marvin Gardens; Paper Moon; Nickelodeon; New York, New York;* and, more recently, *Frances* and *Crackers.* Kovacs describes his involvement with the film: "I had never done anything like this before. That's why I was very excited when Ivan asked me to do it. It was such a challenge because there were so many different facets to it — the magnitude of the visual effects, the 65mm format and so forth.

"There was pretty close communication among Ivan, Richard Edlund [ASC], who was the supervisor of special effects, his matte painters and artists, and myself. There were actual sketches available to all of us to give us a very strong idea of what to expect and create. Everybody has to have an idea of what's going on in the scenes, especially the gaffer; certain things had to be pre-planned and set up, lighting-wise. Without the storyboards, we couldn't have done that. For example, I used the largest arcs ever built in Hollywood. They built 16 of them, and I used 14! I had specially built shutters for the arcs because we needed to simulate a lightning effect. So every shot had to be very carefully designed."

Photographing *Ghostbusters* indeed presented its own set of problems. The situations that arise in the film, and which are humorous to the viewer, are taken very seriously by the characters. Therefore, the filming was done as though the film were a drama, not a comedy. "I am grateful to Ivan," says Kovacs, "because the first thing he told me — and I love him for it! — was that he didn't want this film to look like a comedy. He wanted it to look like a dramatic piece of film. Afterwards I realized it was really a great approach, and it made tremendous sense.

"Automatically, everybody shoots comedy in the traditional way: very high-key photography, bright, cheerful and all that. I've done other comedies before and, for various reasons, I have always followed the old, traditional way of lighting comedy. But when you think of it, comedy is really a piece of drama. It is, in fact, harder to do than drama, especially a film [about] ghosts getting loose in New York, which is kind of a silly idea. If you don't treat it seriously visually, as you would a drama, it's not going to have any credibility."

Reitman had approached Columbia with the project in May of 1983. By June the film was set to go, the only problem being that the studio insisted the film be ready for an early summer 1984 release, so that it would be in theaters well before the Olympic games. This was especially difficult in light of the large quantity of special effects — almost 200 shots. Fortunately, the production was able to enlist the skills of Edlund's newly established Boss Film Company effects house, where most people, including visual-effects arts director John Bruno, had previously worked on *Poltergeist*, giving them prior experience in handling ghosts.

Unlike live action, which was shot in the normal 35mm format, the film's special effects were shot using 65mm. This, in turn, confronted Kovacs with new problems. "At times it was like a horror story!" he recalls. "It was very difficult because of the amount of light required by the 65mm format. Not only that, but the [effects] people needed as much depth of field as I could give them. That way the unseen third dimension they create later on looks more believable. And for them to be able to match my work, I had to establish a certain light level and stay with it. I tried to understand their problems, and there were some really brilliant people there. I hadn't had this kind of experience before, and I learned a lot from them.

"There was always the problem of compromise, because ideally you light for one angle. But when you have two or three angles, and especially close-ups, it's very difficult, because you have to make a multiple choice. In a long shot the face is fully lit, but you create all kinds of other shadow areas in the frame. Then, when you cut to the close-up, you have to create the same shadows and the same kind of a feeling. If it's a fully lit face, it doesn't work and won't match the intercuts. Hence, the necessity of creating a compromise. You really have to light the close-up in the long shot, as refined as if you were doing the close-up separately. I figured out a way, which was to do the close-ups at the very end. That way we could refine it. It was very interesting and, at times, it was really a problem."

Another problem Kovacs faced was that the 65mm cameras always had to be locked off because of the registration problem. "That made the coverage very difficult," says the cinematographer. "Ivan asked me to utilize two 35mm cameras and, whenever I could, cover the scene in a close-up and a medium shot simultaneously, or shoot a full shot and medium shot, depending on how he wanted to present the action. The 35mm cameras had to exclude the angle that the 65mm cameras saw, where the ghost would eventually be; otherwise it would show up in the 35mm angle. The coverage was very difficult, but after a while we got it down almost to a science."

In addition to the skills of Edlund, Bruno and the other Boss Film people, *Ghostbusters* was fortunate to enlist the talents of John De Cuir as production designer. De Cuir has been in the business since the 1940s, and his credits include *The King and I*, *Cleopatra* and *Hello, Dolly!* De Cuir's most difficult task on *Ghostbusters* was the designing of the Gozer Temple set on Stage 16 at Burbank Studios. This set, which was 60' tall, covered the entire stage. It represented the top of a Manhattan apartment building and was surrounded by a backlit, 360-degree panoramic backdrop featuring the New York skyline.

"Shooting was especially difficult on Stage 16, where a lot of 65mm effects had to be shot," Kovacs continues. "One day we had two or three 65mm cameras and three 35mm cameras lined up, doing the same setup. I had to basically light for the 65mm in order to achieve the stop they preferred, which was T5.6. But in certain situations I wasn't able to give them more than T4 due to physical conditions.

"The set presented an enormous logistics problem. For instance, Colin Campbell, my gaffer, built light racks behind the painted New York backing, which was over 400 feet long and 60 feet high. There were 7,500 300-watt mushroom globes strategically located behind windows [in the backdrop]. Even the Central Park lamps were little Christmas lights! That gave depth and life to a basically immobile backing. The rigging of that stage alone took six weeks. The rigging — equipment rentals, cables, generators, et cetera — cost $300,000, and that was without labor. It was supposed to look real, so we did a lot of tests with different degrees of light intensity coming through the windows and lighting the sky. And for a while, nothing worked! But miraculously, the day before shooting, on the last test, we came up with something that we thought was really believable."

According to Kovacs, *Ghostbusters* shot on Stage 16 for 21 days. Both he and assistant producer Michael Gross remember the period as the most difficult part of the production, because of the size of the set and the technical nature of the visual effects. "It required so many big lighting units," says Kovacs. "I hardly had any thing smaller than 10Ks; I only had a few 5Ks, which I used on the foreground action. We had 14 Titans, regular 10K arcs, and huge, old-fashioned Big Eye 10Ks. The whole studio has the capacity to supply 80,000 amps, and we needed 50,000! They could only give us 15,000 amps, even when the neighboring productions gave all their power to us. So Stage 16 was surrounded by huge generators rented from Disney, Fox, Paramount and independent rental companies, whoever had generators. We had 12 separate vehicles generating power whenever we turned on the lights!

"This is a good example of why a close relationship with the gaffer is very important on a film like this. You have to know, months ahead of time, that in certain areas you will need so-called 'hot' 10Ks. They have hot lenses that refocus and collect the light, giving off a smaller, narrower beam, but you have a bigger intensity from the same distance. In this case we needed both the wide coverage and the high intensity, so we mixed one hot lens and one wide lens.

"The reason we had to use those huge units was that due to the largeness of the sets, the light had to travel more distance, and it had to be of overpowering intensity. It was a struggle. Plus, sometimes we had to put a green gel, a red gel, an orange or a pink in front of the light, depending on what was happening at that moment in the sky with the ghosts."

Kovacs is very complimentary about De Cuir's contributions. "He's a great, brilliant artist," he says. "All of our lights were 60 feet above ground. At the end of the stairway on the set is Gozer's pyramid. Its peak was right at the rafters, and on top of the pyramid, I needed another Titan. We figured that the only way we could do it would be to take out the rafters and put in a bed, which is hung from the ceiling, and put the Titan there. But we only had to do that for that one light. John De Cuir went over things very carefully with me and my gaffer [in order] to leave us places for the lights. He always created every set keeping in mind how it should be lit. He provided little architectural elements where we could hide lights, and a little visual interest that would catch a little more light, or some kind of a texture.

"The idea was to use a strong backlight on the whole stairway, and also use crosslight. First of all, I had to build the stop up to about T16, because when the ghost appears, we wanted to create an overexposed effect, with everything bathed in light. I had to give the 65mm camera a stop of T8. I used the same stop on my [35mm] camera, but it needed two more stops overexposure. That's why I needed the tremendous amount of power. Also, creating the backlight effect is really not using the full extent of the lights. If you frontlight you achieve overexposure much sooner. It's very difficult to overexpose with crosslight and backlight."

Portions of *Ghostbusters* were shot on location in New York City, where the production used an actual building to represent the locale of the Gozer temple. The building was later enhanced in several shots through the use of mattes and other opticals. Lighting differences between Los Angeles and New York were another problem Kovacs had to face. "I had three lighting crews for this picture. I had a New York gaffer, Billy Ward, who was wonderful. I had a California gaffer, Colin Campbell, plus we had a rigging crew that was actually larger than the two shooting crews combined.

"Shooting [in both cities] at night is no trouble, because you create your own atmospheric conditions with smoke and backlight. But during the day, the light [in each city] looks different. First of all, New York is very far north, and during wintertime the arc of the sun is much lower, creating a much more pleasing light, as opposed to the even winter light in Southern California. The higher the light is, the uglier it is, especially on the face. The low-arc sun gives you wonderful backlight. So I try to stage the action in backlight, or shoot from a certain direction. Ivan was always very helpful [in making this possible].

"There were situations, however, when I had trouble making an exact match, and where we had to drop a few shots and redo them here in Los Angeles. On the close shots, you can silk it and control the sunlight if a huge area isn't involved. There were quite a few scenes that took place in front of the Gozer building that we didn't shoot in New York, but here on the Columbia backlot. The building was built to the second floor, and wide enough so that we could do some smaller scenes, and I had to silk the whole area."

In the case of *Ghostbusters*, Kovacs' first real brush with a giant, special effects-laden production, the challenges were met with considerable success in spite of the pressures of a very short schedule. The difficulties encountered once again prove the necessity of collaboration.

First published in *American Cinematographer*, June 1984.

From left: director Martin Scorsese, an unidentified crew member, camera operator Robert Stevens, Kovacs (at camera) and 1st assistant camera Joe Thibomaneuver through a nightclub entranceway lit with 1,600 bulbs during filming of *New York, New York* (1977).

6

Laszlo Kovacs Teaches Lighting

by

Jon Silberg

During the past several years, Laszlo Kovacs, ASC has conducted an annual lighting seminar under the auspices of the UCLA extension program. Some 80 students participated in the 1998 seminar, which was conducted on a soundstage at the Panavision facility in Woodland Hills, California. Panavision provided the stage, camera and lighting equipment; Kodak provided the film, and Deluxe Hollywood provided the processing.

The seminar was staged during two weekends. During the first weekend Kovacs demonstrated lighting techniques in a range of situations. The following weekend Kovacs and the students watched dailies. The most important lessons he taught focused on why he made decisions regarding lighting and the selection of lens, filtration and diffusion.

Kovacs lit actors in a variety of situations to demonstrate how light can be manipulated to create a sense of time and place, in addition to evoking emotional responses. As he lit each scene, Kovacs shared anecdotes about the lessons he has learned over the years, first working with Roger Corman on a minimalist form of filmmaking ("All the equipment we had fit into one station wagon.") and later working with directors such as Bob Rafelson (*Five Easy Pieces*), Hal Ashby (*Shampoo)*, Peter Bogdanovich (*Paper Moon)* and P.J. Hogan (*My Best Friend's Wedding*). The common thread woven through the fabric of his dialogue, was the importance of controlling light. His first point of reference was *Easy Rider*, which was on the leading edge of a new wave of reality filmmaking.

"Everyone asks me what it was like shooting *Easy Rider*," he said. "Almost everyone assumes that we took almost a defiant approach to filmmaking and simply shot what was happening in front of the camera. The truth is that each scene was carefully planned; nothing was left to chance. You have to control the look of what you shoot, and the way to do that is by lighting it properly."

Kovacs noted that film and lens technologies have come a long way since he shot *Easy Rider*. In those days, the only film speed was 50 ASA. While most labs offered custom push-processes, there was a penalty in heightened graininess. For the UCLA workshop, he used

Kodak Vision 500T 5279 film stock, but he cautioned students that fast film is not a substitute for diligence in lighting.

"There is a lot of pressure on cinematographers today to set up and work faster because of the high cost of making films," he said. "Fast film and lenses will get you a proper exposure at low key levels and even in natural light, but that isn't cinematography. Cinematography is the art of using light and color like words and punctuation. The more skillful you are at controlling light, the better you are at expressing your artistic instincts."

Kovacs walked the class through the process of creating artificial sunlight, candlelight and light at various other color temperatures. He said his preference is to shoot at a constant stop of T4 whenever possible, because that's the sweet spot of most lenses and captures a sense of depth. He also discussed the differences between shooting with spherical and anamorphic lenses. His preference is anamorphic. "I get asked why I prefer anamorphic by directors and producers who haven't worked in that format," he said. "My strategy is to get them to shoot a test comparing formats. They usually look at the dailies of the test with me and come to the conclusion that anamorphic really does look more like a movie."

Kovacs used a pre-digital Spectra light meter aimed at the light source, not the lens, and he measured T-stops rather than footcandles. While he stressed the importance of metering, Kovacs said, "Trust your eye. It's the most important, most accurate meter available."

Kovacs also explained why fill light is important. Because of today's fast films and lenses, he noted that proper use of fill is often ignored. He said that some people don't understand that the use of fill light is a creative decision. "If it's too low the ambient lighting gets in the way, and if it's too high the difference between the highs and lows are not pronounced enough."

The second weekend, the class watched projected film dailies in a screening room as Kovacs provided a running commentary on each setup. He pointed out differences between the quality of images projected on the screen and video images. "You can see subtle differences in lighting and filtration [on film] that aren't apparent on video monitors. That's a problem even on the set, where a lot of directors are trained to look at the video-tap monitor instead of what's happening on the set. It's not only misleading in terms of light and colors, but also in terms of framing — you see directors looking at a small video screen, asking for tighter and tighter shots without realizing how that will look on the big screen."

The moral: like it or not, many directors are going to eschew film dailies, so be prepared to explain the shortcomings of the video monitor and never rely on it yourself. Kovacs added, "You have to know each emulsion that you choose to work with and how it reacts to light and colors. You should know what the film is going to look like *before* you see dailies."

Kovacs also addressed the issue of working with first-time directors. He said it doesn't faze him, and he encouraged the cinematographers in the audience to keep an open mind. "It takes a lot for anyone to get to the point where he can get out there on a set and say

'Action.' I've found that new directors can bring excitement and enthusiasm and something unique to a film."

Many people attending the seminar were digital artists and compositors from visual-effects facilities. Kovacs noted that modern digital technology enables people who work in postproduction to alter aesthetic decisions involving framing, camera movement, lighting and contrast, which were once the cinematographer's exclusive domain. "Unless you're a better cinematographer than Vilmos Zsigmond, don't attempt to interpret his work," he observed. "It's encouraging that so many of you are in this workshop. I think that it's important for you to understand what we do and why."

Kovacs noted that the relationship between cinematographers and post artists is a two-way street. "People I know at post houses tell me they welcome cinematographers to come around to their facilities when they are compositing shots, and only a few of them do. I personally can't imagine walking away from a picture before it's complete. A new era is opening in digital effects, and we all have to work very closely." Kovacs noted that on *Multiplicity*, he and visual-effects supervisor Richard Edlund, ASC conferred daily, and he shot all of the green- and bluescreen elements himself.

Kovacs recalled that during the early days of his career, many veteran cinematographers were not willing to share information with younger colleagues; he, on the other hand, welcomes opportunities to do so. "Teaching a seminar like this helps me to re-examine my own thinking. I'm teaching, and I'm also learning."

Michael Keaton in front a the greenscreen setup on the set of *Multiplicity* (1996).

7

Send in the Clones

Laszlo Kovacs, ASC works with Richard Edlund, ASC
and Boss Film to create a menagerie of Michael Keatons in *Multiplicity.*

by

Les Paul Robley

In Columbia Pictures' *Multiplicity*, too many commitments and not enough time are problems for Doug Kinney (Michael Keaton). With work, family and personal needs all vying for his attention, Doug decides to become the ultimate split personality by having himself cloned three times. Naturally, this decision creates trouble for Doug; but the fictional dilemma also caused craziness for the film's production crew.

To achieve this film's slapstick scenario, director Harold Ramis (*Groundhog Day*) called upon the expertise of cinematographer Laszlo Kovacs, ASC, effects wizard Richard Edlund, ASC and Boss Film. Working together, the *Multiplicity* team was able to present up to four Michael Keatons onscreen at the same time, creating the illusion of four identical actors playing distinctly different characters throughout the film.

"I welcomed the idea very much," says Kovacs, whose credits range from the anti-establishment classic *Easy Rider* to the recent thriller *Copycat.* "I had worked with [Ramis and Edlund] before, on the first *Ghostbusters.* But back then everything was optical, and now everything is digital. This film presented some interesting and different problems to solve. The digital process is so natural that it seemed as if the script had been invented for it."

Multiplicity was the kind of project that required the presence of the visual-effects supervisor for every effects shot. And in that role, Edlund had input on physical action, shot blocking and whether the use of greenscreen was required to replace a background digitally. But as Kovacs notes with good cheer, "I had to execute it. This film is a perfect example of a close working relationship between a visual-effects supervisor and a cinematographer."

The cinematic approach for the clone sequences was to cover and block the scenes as if there were, in fact, four different actors playing four different parts. The production used wide master shots that would include all four characters, plus conventional over-the-shoulder singles and two-shots that included each of them at least once.

During preparation, it was decided that all scenes in which the clones appeared together would be storyboarded. This was done so that the studio would know how much the scenes would cost and how many composites were needed, and so Keaton could understand the rough structure of the scenes. The boards also enabled the digital-effects artists to position Keaton appropriately and create convincing composites. "It was very complicated for Michael," Kovacs attests. "Many times he was carrying an entire sequence because there were no other actors involved. Mentally, he was so tired that sometimes by five o'clock he would say, 'I can't do it anymore. I've totally lost it.' So we'd leave everything and go home.

"Sometimes we changed the storyboards when Harold [Ramis] felt that a scene [worked so well in one shot] that it didn't require any further coverage. For the sofa scene, for example, we showed all three clones and Doug, and there was no reason to cut it for coverage. It played so credibly because the characters had physical interaction with each other."

In addition to elaborate storyboards, on-set rehearsals were needed to aid Kovacs in lighting the set and to help Edlund's crew determine the best blocking for the final composites. "We had stand-ins for each of the different characters Michael was playing," recalls Kovacs. "He would play against them to determine the blocking and get an idea of where he would take the scene. For each particular setup, he'd first play the main character, whichever one drove the scene. Then they'd switch parts. If Michael tried playing Clone 2 and found that it wasn't working well for him, we'd go back and change the situation or the blocking. This process would then go down the line to Clones 3 and 4. Many times it took the better part of the day just to rehearse a scene and make sure that it felt good for the actor, the director, and also for me."

It was very important to have Keaton's movements choreographed down to the last detail, because they could dictate the lighting for a scene. "We could not have any shadow contamination from one pass to the next," says Kovacs, "because it would be almost impossible to match during subsequent passes. Boss would have had to do something digitally in post, which would have created a major expense in terms of time and money. Harold gave me tremendous freedom in terms of making suggestions and offering ideas if I felt there were potential problems in a scene — say, if actors were maybe too close to one another, and the casting of shadows was unavoidable. Richard was also very helpful in solving these problems. Once I decided how I was going to light the scene and we put down the first pass, I couldn't change anything. I couldn't add an extra fill light, tweak a key or even replace a burnout due to [the possibility of] light contamination."

Kovacs could only change a light when there was a greenscreen background, and that area had not been part of a previous pass. In such situations he could make adjustments by examining a freeze-frame taken of the previous pass, but those instances were extremely rare. "When I said I was ready, I was prepared to commit myself 100 percent until I saw the final result," he adds, noting that the "final" stage was usually many months down the line.

During prep, Kovacs scouted locations and met with production designer Jack DeGovia, a process that provided him an overall strategy for the look and texture of the film. He explains, "I felt that the most important thing for this story, even though it is a comedy, was to give it a sense of credibility, a real environment, real sources and sets and real situations. Because of that, I tried to follow the sources very strongly. If there was a window, I made sure the window became the source. If there were practicals such as table lamps, we strove for the best possible lamp to follow the source of that type of light. This happens throughout the course of a normal shoot, but this was not a normal shoot. On this project, 'normality' had a totally different meaning.

"Then there were the possible shadow problems when the actors started moving. To me it was not always very visible, because during rehearsals the stand-ins were not always doing things the way Michael might later on. He often changed things [on the set], and those changes weren't included in my plan. So I was concerned that when he was doing something with his hands, they might cast a wrong shadow or go through a source and ruin the shot. At the same time, the scene had to look very real. If you don't create a reality for this kind of visual trickery, the audience is going to become very suspicious and wonder how it was done."

During preproduction, the filmmakers made another important decision concerning location exteriors, such as the house where Doug and his wife (Andie MacDowell) live. The actual Pasadena location included a two-story family home with a long driveway and the façade of a guesthouse (where the clones hide from Doug's wife) placed above the garage. These exteriors established tie-in shots of the clones arriving, or the wife leaving the house. However, there were also many scenes involving Doug and all three clones in the backyard and inside the house. These could not be made on location because if the light changed, the consistency between one pass and the next could be jeopardized.

"You can't have four different color backgrounds," Kovacs points out, "so we had to duplicate that whole property on massive Stage 15 at Sony Studios. The set was in one-to-one scale, though we shortened the distance a bit between the garage and the main building.

"The big problem in recreating a daylight exterior is duplicating a single-source sunlight effect. I didn't want to see a person walking and two or three shadows following him. That's an immediate giveaway. So I used huge Mole-Richardson 20K spotlights, which have a very powerful, even, widespread beam. I used three major angles when I was covering the backside of the house to the garage, where wide action was occurring.

"The Number Two 20K wasn't wide enough to cover the backyard garage," he notes. "But [production designer] Jack DeGovia came up with the idea of adding an arbor about 12 feet away from the garage building, exactly where the edge of one lamp was giving way to another. That idea worked wonderfully and saved me from having the double shadow. Plus, the huge tree built in the middle of the courtyard scattered any shadow problems."

The very first visual-effects shot for *Multiplicity* was filmed at the new Skirball Institute in Los Angeles, where Doug is introduced to the cloning process. The location proved to be a pandemonium of construction equipment and cables because the new institute was still under construction.

The shot involved each of the axis components of a Kuper motion-control system: a dolly, boom, pan, tilt and focus change. As a result, the floor became a rat's nest of motion-control servo cables, video lines and encoder cables. I served as motion-control operator throughout the 100-day shoot, with Landen Ruddell and Bill Klinger as dolly technicians. Servo motors were chosen to power the dolly and gear head for quiet operation during live sound recordings. Jeff Platt and Donny Sierer were the electronics techs who put it all together in sync with the Panavision camera, Pro Tools time code, motion-control rigs and Silicon Graphics (SGI) computer workstations (situated in a mobile trailer outside the institute due to possible noise contamination from tile computer fans and hard-drives).

Klinger and Ruddell used machinist's gauges mounted on a heavy steel track to make sure the friction-wheeled dolly always started from the same position for every take. Since a friction-pinch roller was needed to reduce the noise one would get from a standard mo-co belt-driven system, shots could only be made while moving in one direction. The crew compensated for backlash by rolling the dolly slightly farther in one direction, then moving it back in the direction of travel to set a zero home position.

Rough rehearsals were accomplished with Preston either pushing the dolly by hand (an encoder on the wheel recorded the curvature of the move), or using a Hot Wheels arrangement (similar to a pan-tilt Hothead) that actuated the dolly and boom. The actual movement was calibrated in inches, and I set software limits to prevent the dolly from overshooting its mark and rolling off edge of the track or banging into a wall. Sometimes we would squeeze or stretch the dolly move to make it stop or roll beyond a selected point, depending on what Ramis or Kovacs wanted during rehearsals.

When it came time to roll film for an actual first pass, the dolly was operated by the encoder wheels (as were tile pan, tilt, boom and focus), with joystick limits set for maximum smoothing so that the track would slam into its end position each time without fail. This was done because the dolly could not repeat a pass exactly when pushed manually, since slight variations in friction slippage would occur. The dolly was only dead-on when operated remotely by Hothead control, because any slippage would repeat by the same amount for subsequent passes. (This was ascertained during field chart tests at the prep stage.)

Once a circled take was laid down on the Kuper RTMC130 software, a move could not be changed or smoothed in any way. Even the focus axis (recorded by first AC Zoran Veselic) and the pan and tilt (operated by Michael Stone) could not be adjusted, since any discrep-

Easy Rider (1969). Kovacs was filming the "rides" from an open convertible using a telephoto lens and rack focus on an Arri IIC camera.

Easy Rider (1969). Peter Fonda as Captain America and Jack Nicholson as alcoholic lawyer George Hansen. Nicholson was nominated for an Academy Award for Best Supporting Actor.

The Last Movie (1971). Kovacs testing out a rig for an aerial shot.

New York, New York (1977). Liza Minelli gets her happy ending.

New York, New York (1977). Liza Minelli and Robert DeNiro riff at his audition.

A summit meeting of top cinematographers in the early 1970s. Left to right: Vittorio Storaro, ASC, AIC, Vilmos Zsigmond, ASC, director Mark Rydell, Billy Williams, BSC and Laszlo Kovacs, ASC.

PHOTO: SIDNEY BALDWIN

Free Willy 2 (1995). The dolphin wrangler feeds the stars of the film.

F.I.S.T. (1978). Sylvester Stallone shown in a classically composed dramatic moment.

F.I.S.T. (1978). Dramatic lighting characterizes this period drama about union workers.

PHOTO: MARC SCHREIBMAN

The Legend of the Lone Ranger (1981). The Masked Marvel and Tonto posed before a number of different backgrounds for this publicity shot.

Kovacs sets up for an exterior shot while filming *The Lone Ranger* (1981).

PHOTO: STEPHEN VAUGHAN

Kovacs during filming of *Multiplicity* (1996).

Multiplicity (1996). Michael Keaton is shown with the greenscreen setup and the video monitor he used to time his movements on camera.

PHOTO: CHRIS HELECERMANAS-BENGE

Return to Me (2000). David Duchovny and Minnie Driver reconcile in this romantic comedy.

PHOTO: RON BATZDORFF

Miss Congeniality (2000). Michael Caine and stumblebum Sandra Bullock take a walk.

PHOTO: RON BATZDORFF

Miss Congeniality (2000). William Shatner hosting a beauty pageant with the assembled contestants.

ancy would mismatch the original take played back by the SGI computers.

A first pass proceeded as follows: Pro Tools operator Peter Brancaccio began the time code, which was hard-wired to mo-co and the SGI machines with a 20-second countdown. The camera rolled at 10 seconds, and sync lock was established via a Panavision-to-Kuper sync cable preset to 24 frames in the software. The time code trigger point was input at 00:00:20:04 seconds (the :04 frames resulted as a consistent offset). A bloop light attached to the video time code slate (operated by second AC Michael Gurasich) signaled the first frame of mo-co movement on film and video. This sync point was later used to realign all subsequent digital passes in postproduction at Boss, and as a checkpoint for real-time traveling split playback on the set to make sure everyone was in sync.

Boss Film's real-time traveling split process was developed by Gautham Krishnamurti, Shahril Ibrahim and Hiro Miyoshi. "The software enabled us to play back video off the SGI computers and blend it at the same time with incoming video, compositing them together using some kind of chroma-key or luma-key function," explains Krishnamurti.

"Seeing composites in real time was not only great for the director and Michael to check eye level, but also for me," admits Kovacs. "I had to check for shadows and problems that might occur in the subsequent takes. When we saw a problem in the second or third pass, the only thing we could do was change his placement slightly to avoid a shadow crossover or green spill. Only one time were we able to change a light when there was a greenscreen background, because the affected area hadn't yet appeared on a previous pass."

Video monitors synced to time code were sometimes employed to enable Keaton to play against himself while electronic earpieces allowed him to hear his previous dialogue and time his responses.

Once a first pass was recorded and approved by Ramis, nothing in the move or set could be altered. All subsequent passes with Keaton in different roles depended on that original take as the basis for all action. "My crew learned the nature of this type of cinematography very quickly," says Kovacs. "We had to leave the set as a hot set and walk away from it while Michael changed into another character and took on a different personality [and the SGI workstations rotoscoped the traveling splits]."

The camera crew took extra care in changing film magazines so as not to bump the camera in these locked-off positions. Kovacs had to complete all passes on the same film report because of the possibility of day-to-day variations in negative processing at Technicolor. There could be as much as a point difference in color shift, which would cause a problem securing color consistency from one pass to the next. As a result, the crew kept the film until the entire shot of up to four passes was completed; only then would they give it to the lab. "Some days there were no dailies, and the lab wondered if we had taken the day off," Kovacs recalls with a chuckle.

If the crew had to stop between takes, freeze frames were grabbed on the Panasonic

MX-12 video mixer (or recorded on tape) to make certain nothing moved on set or in the camera.

As another precaution, clean passes minus actors — with and without greenscreen — were always made in order to correct mismatches in camera movement, body placement, limb lineups or background contamination. "Clean passes were only helpful for the background, basically," Kovacs reveals. "What happens in the foreground between the characters is that they cast shadows on one another, and then you have a problem. Let's say on the first pass my hand's shadow goes over your arm; when [Michael] plays that clone in a later pass, the stand-in can't match that because he can't see it and doesn't know where it comes from. Stand-ins often held video cameras next to their heads to record Michael's acting, which could be played back just in case he needed it for a particular body movement."

To an outsider, *Multiplicity* must have looked like a very lax production. The crew would often stage basketball tournaments, shoot pool, play pingpong or even take turns with a flight simulator on the SGI machines to relieve the endless waiting. "It took patience," says Kovacs, "and we couldn't afford to slack off because we couldn't make changes after the initial pass, which was usually a half-day's work. We had 50 to 60 people working on each single shot, which isn't normal, especially when you have only one actor in a scene. That tested everyone's patience because everything took a long time. It's very easy to allow mistakes, so you have to be doubly careful. The 60 crew members sometimes seemed to be standing around doing nothing, but when the chips were down, all 60 were suddenly working."

With experience, the Boss Film crew became much faster lining up each complicated effects sequence. But Kovacs was sometimes like a champion steed bursting at the reins on set, waiting for them to set up the camera dolly and Hothead. Asked if this process slowed him down considerably, the veteran cameraman replies, "Not really, because that was all part of the plan. We knew that certain things would take time, and that something to this extent [using real-time traveling mattes] had never been done."

Setting up the motion-control track always took time, because the heavy 10- and 20-foot sections had to be laid out, leveled and cleaned. Additionally, the crew had to mount the dolly, set the gauges and encode the move. For non-dolly shots, the servo-controlled gear head was usually stuck upon a massive iron tripod.

Special circumstances occurred when Keaton entered a room and flipped a lightswitch, or took a shower while an electrical storm flashed through the window. In these cases, practicals and the Lightning Strikes system were controlled via the Kuper editbits function, and sequenced to turn on at the same frame during subsequent passes. For example, if Keaton turned on the light for the first pass, someone watching on set would cue the light gag remotely at the same instant. Later, while the SGI created its splits and Keaton changed costume, Roger Johnson and the mo-co operator determined the exact film frame at which the light came on. This moment was programmed into the Kuper and rigged to light up via computer. A succession of beeps in Keaton's earpiece prompted him to hit the lightswitch again at the appropriate time, if action in the second or third pass required him to do so.

Other unusual situations involved stand-ins wearing greenscreen suits for high-fives and "chest bumps," and the creation of greenscreens with special holes so one character could blow cigarette smoke into a clone's face. These devices enabled Keaton's characters to react with each other very intimately.

Two scenes involved an item being passed from one clone to another. In one, Doug hands a plate of sandwiches to himself; in the other, Doug hands a beer to newly created Clone 3. These scenes employed an arm-replacement technique whereby a stand-in wearing Doug's clothing handed the object to Keaton as Clone 3 in the first pass. The original stand-in's body was matted out, and Keaton was placed in the identical position for the second pass. Keaton, as Doug, later matched his body movement as though he were handing the item to himself. A dolly movement added to the whole effect and helped disguise the trick. However, the perspective change not only made it difficult to line Keaton's body up in the precisely correct position, but also added problems in achieving a safe split.

"[That technique] worked very well in scenes with dynamics of a pan and dolly ending in a three-shot," recalls Kovacs. "When you see all three characters played by the same actor, it creates a fabulous credibility. Many times we tried to avoid scenes involving physical contact or shots of the clones crossing behind one another for budgetary reasons, since we were limited in terms of how many visual effects we could do. Later on, though, we wished we had been bolder because those are the scenes that work really well and don't telegraph to the audience that it's an effects shot."

Kovacs never considered shooting a larger negative, such as VistaVision, to increase the image size for compositing the film's complicated visual effects. In fact, he suggested the use of anamorphic to avoid this prospect altogether. "Anamorphic uses the full 35mm frame from perf to perf, with a very thin frameline on top and bottom," he notes. "That's why the picture quality is so superior to 1.85 and has richer blacks, deeper saturation and better grain and sharpness. I wanted to go with [anamorphic] so we wouldn't have to change formats every time there was an effects shot.

"Another consideration was composition. Because there were as many as four Michael Keatons in one shot, the horizontal frame is very important. We really used the entire field from edge to edge, and I think it will force the video distributor and cable company to either letterbox the film or lose half the action. This film should really test the philosophy of showing full-frame to a cable audience."

In running down his choice of lenses, Kovacs relates, "I originally started with Panavision Primo lenses, then went to regular C- and E-Series lenses." He abandoned the Primo lenses, even though they are considered optically sharper than the C- and E-Series units, because he did not want a microscopically sharp image that reproduced every pore or defect on the skin. That's why the Tiffen Soft/FX-2 filter is a particular favorite of his. "In close-ups, it gives a slight diffusion on faces and skin tones. I consider the Soft/FX series of filters to be magical; they really don't affect sharpness or contrast, but they hide little blemishes on the skin, especially on female portraits. I used a Soft/FX on every single shot because I didn't want to add another variable to the visual-effects roster, which could add to confusion for the eye.

"From my previous picture, *Copycat*, I had a set of perfectly matched C- and E-Series lenses which went from 35mm to 100mm. But I still had a major problem with the series, because with prime lenses of 40mm, 50mm, 75mm, 85mm and 100mm, I was missing an important focal length between 50mm and 75mm. A 50mm has a slightly wide-angle look, and a 75mm is already on the larger end of the focal length. I needed a 60mm, and I kept begging Panavision to make me one."

Two months into production, Panavision's Phil Radin and Larry Hezzelwood showed up on the set with a brand-new lens box bearing Kovacs' name. Inside was their gift to *Multiplicity*: a C-Series 60mm lens.

Kovacs had asked DeGovia to make all of the film's interiors 25 percent larger than normal. "The dolly movement and character placement inside was very important," he said. "With the right lens, you can make [the space] look either bigger or shorter. The 60mm lens was like a blessing, because suddenly we had the answer. When a shot required all four clones, obviously I had to use a wide-angle lens. I couldn't use a 75mm because it was too tight. Even a 50mm was a compromise because it was too wide with anamorphic. We would have had to foreshorten the distances so the guesthouse set wouldn't look like Grand Central Station!"

Kovacs also kept his aperture consistent, working at T4 throughout the show except while doing motion-control dolly moves; in those situations he would increase it for the extra depth of field, as everything that had to do with the camera was unalterable, including focus.

Such considerations also dictated Kovacs' choice of film stocks. He used Eastman Kodak EXR 5298 for all greenscreen applications and EXR 5296 for all non-greenscreen interiors. "My decision at the beginning was to use the 96 because the quality gives you a softer rendition of the spectrum and a lower contrast ratio than 98. I later discovered that the 96 is very close to 98; when we used the 98 with greenscreen, the other scenes that were shot on the 96 in the same sequence came out on the same printing light. The dailies looked identical.

"When Kodak introduces a stock, they constantly improve it. If it lacks in contrast, blacks or saturation, they improve it with each batch. They have perfected the 96 so that it has the fine-grain structure of 98. When we did the compositing between the shots made on 96 and those shot on 98, they came out with very much the same printing lights.

Also, the contrast ratio was nearly identical. I could have used 98 all the way through, except for the exteriors."

Pondering the image quality of film that has been digitally recorded for effects work, Kovacs notes, "There is a very slight quality change — I don't use the word 'loss' — when you go through the digital compositing process and match to the original camera negative. But you can digitally manipulate the contrast level to match the original 96 negative. After the test sessions, we went back and really nit-picked the fine details when we had more time.

"There are two areas which are very critical: contrast and grain [or sharpness]," continues Kovacs. "So far, we've only had to re-do four shots out of 40, which is very good. Bob Kaiser, my answer-print timer for many years, was very impressed. He told me we only had to worry about those two areas because they're the factors we can't change.

"Basically, my negative was very consistent in the one-light workprint, so [the lab] didn't have the problem of having to correct one side against the other. That made it very easy and very fast so they could concentrate on the splits and mattes. Even when we do an initial eyeline test composite, I'm really surprised because the contrast, sharpness and color are all very good to start with, and I haven't had to touch the color."

Despite the exacting nature of this production, Kovacs says he would gladly return for a *Multiplicity* sequel. "Waiting for the special effects was not a problem," he asserts. "It was simply important to have patience and understand the nature of the beast."

First published in *American Cinematographer*, June 1996.

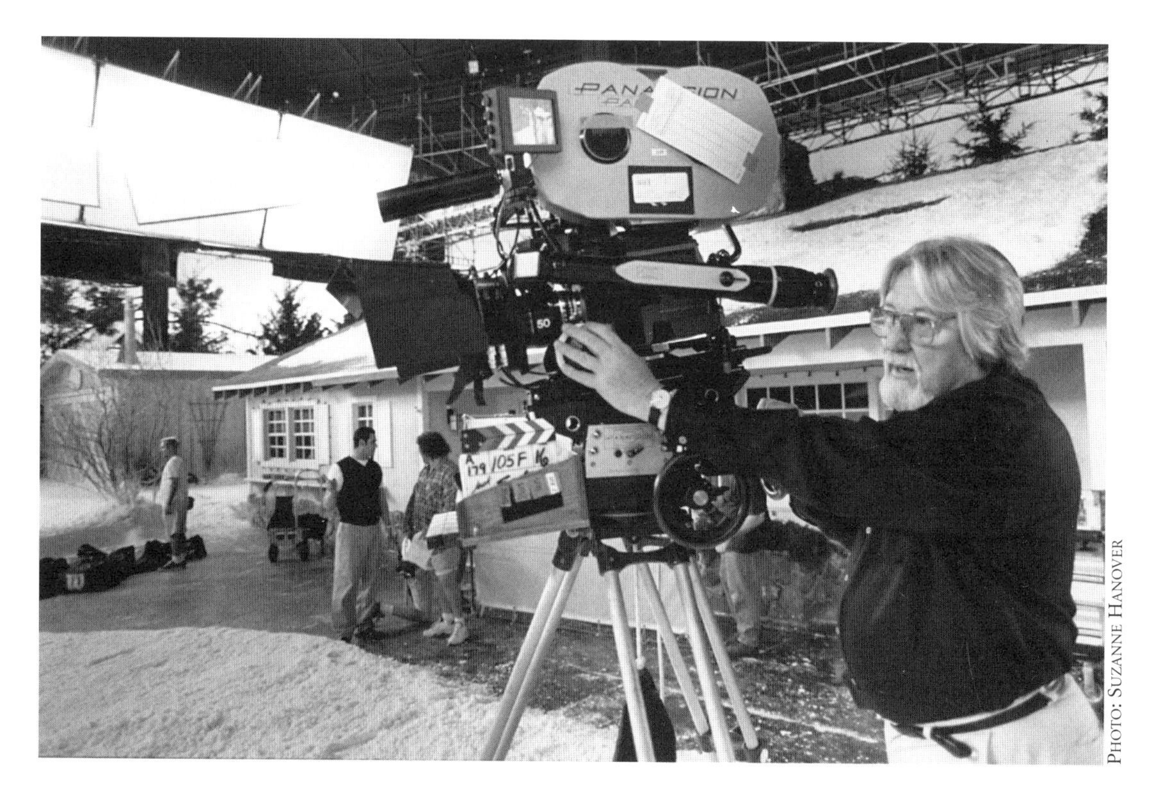

PHOTO: SUZANNE HANOVER

Kovacs on the set of *Jack Frost* (1998).

8

Laszlo Kovacs Shoots *Jack Frost*, a Film About a Dream Come True

by

Bob Fisher

Jack Frost is an impossible dream come true. The story is a modern-day fable about a snowman who comes to life and helps a 10-year-old boy named Charlie through an extremely difficult time. The boy's father, portrayed by Michael Keaton, is a likable but overly ambitious jazz musician who neglects his family while pursuing his own career. Despite Charlie's pleas, the father leaves home on Christmas Eve for a gig at a festival run by a record producer. He is killed in an auto accident while attempting to drive home during a blizzard. His untimely death leaves a gaping hole in Charlie's life.

The next Christmas Eve, Charlie builds a snowman in the front yard of his home. That's where the magic begins. Charlie soon discovers that his father has returned as the snowman. It's as though they are being given a second chance.

If this sounds slightly familiar, chances are you are remembering a character many of us met in childhood storybooks and in a song: "Frosty the Snowman."

The film's opening scene establishes the father's identity. It was filmed in an old movie palace that has been converted into a dance hall. The scene opens with a wide exterior shot on the street, across the street from the theater. Falling snow was created in a digital suite and composited into the exterior footage. The camera glides smoothly on a Steadicam through traffic, across the street, into the cinema, up and down steps and into a crowd, until suddenly there is a small opening that reveals a stage where Keaton's character and his band are performing. The camera moves through couples dancing in the foreground and finally comes in for a tight close-up on Keaton's face. This single shot lasts for about three minutes. The music is a rock version of "Frosty the Snowman" and Keaton, coached by the band, does his own singing.

Jack Frost was photographed by Laszlo Kovacs, ASC and directed by Troy Miller. It is Miller's first outing on a feature film; his previous credits include the MOW *Beverly Hills Family Robinson* and other TV programs. He made his mark during a recent Academy Awards broadcast with a comedic short film that placed Billy Crystal in scenes from films nominated for Best Picture.

Michael Tadross, one of *Jack Frost*'s producers, introduced Miller to Kovacs and suggested that it was important to have an experienced cinematographer on this project. Miller's first reaction was skepticism; he asked Kovacs why he was interested in shooting his little film about a snowman and a child. Kovacs assured Miller that was exactly what interested him. "*Jack Frost* is an allegory, which was brilliantly interpreted by Troy," says Kovacs. "It's a reminder to all parents that it's important to show your love for your children today, because sometimes tomorrow never comes."

That might sound corny, but as the father of a 10-year-old girl, Kovacs says the idea of making a film that parents can take their pre-teen children to resonated with him. He looked forward to that experience.

Jack Frost was produced by The Canton Company and Warner Bros. and is based on an original script by Jeff Cesario and Mark Steven Johnson. "Every successful movie begins with the vision of the director," Kovacs says, "but it takes a team effort to make a film like this. That includes the producers, who believed in what we were doing, as well as the cast and crew."

The making of *Jack Frost* presented some formidable technical and creative challenges. Should it be a cartoon or comic-book version of reality, or a drama with threads of comedy running through the fabric of the story? How do you make audiences believe that a fictional snowman looks and feels real enough for them to cross the threshold of disbelief and temporarily embrace a fantasy? More than a few recent sci-fi films which much bigger budgets have foundered on that treacherous shore.

Kovacs is the same cinematographer who was dubbed king of the American New Wave after filming *Easy Rider* just 30 years ago. In that landmark film, Peter Fonda, Jack Nicholson and Dennis Hopper portrayed burn-outs searching for the American dream in the midst of the 1960s drug culture. It was a cutting-edge exercise in minimalist filmmaking.

Jack Frost was filmed at locations in and around Truckee, California, but most of it was shot on a 200'x300' soundstage in a former airplane hangar in Long Beach that once housed Howard Hughes' *Spruce Goose*. The main set simulated the exteriors of five homes on the street where Charlie and his family live. The street was extended on either side with huge TransLites. There were a few other sets on the stage, where Kovacs estimates that some 60 percent of the principal photography was done.

Jack Frost was shot in the 35mm anamorphic format even though much of the story focuses on the relationship between two characters, and one of them is fictional. Kelly

Preston plays Charlie's mother, who is kept in the dark about her son's relationship with the snowman. The snowman is played by an actor inside a snowman costume with the aid of puppeteers, and some digital magic provided by Industrial Light & Magic.

"All of us know people like Charlie's father," says Kovacs. "He's a good person who works so hard that he neglects his family. He's not even aware that Charlie is an excellent player on the school hockey team. He's never seen a game. Halfway to a Christmas job, Charlie's dad becomes remorseful and decides to drive home in the middle of a storm. He's thinking about being with his family on Christmas when he loses control of the car, goes off a bridge and dies."

Shooting an anamorphic project was a new experience for Miller, who has always worked within the constraints of the TV screen. Kovacs spoke with Miller about the aesthetics of using the 2.4:1 image to keep the audience engaged. "Basically, this story takes place in snow country, with beautiful mountains, valleys and vistas in the background," Kovacs says. "I saw the house early on in preproduction. It was 80 feet wide with a big front yard, and there were similar houses on either side and across the street."

Kovacs told Miller that they could create a more intimate story in the anamorphic format, which goes against conventional wisdom. He says, "We see the world horizontally and move our heads from left to right, not up and down. The snowman is much taller than the boy and both of them are vertical, which makes them great counterpoints in horizontal frames." He advised Miller, "Watch any John Ford movie and look at how he used space."

A second and equally compelling rationale is that anamorphic movies, when properly composed, feel more cinematic to the audience.

Kovacs says that he learned an invaluable lesson early in his career during a conversation with Orson Welles, whom he met while shooting *Paper Moon* with Peter Bogdanovich. Welles suggested avoiding cutaways because they interrupt the story. Kovacs counts that advice as a formative experience that he applied in *Jack Frost*. Much of the story is told in two-shots with the environment playing a role.

Miller embraced the widescreen concept. He immediately began refining storyboards to reflect a 2.4:1 aspect ratio instead of 1.85:1. Within days, the director told Kovacs that the wider format had added a layer to the creative process and offered much richer images and more sophisticated staging of scenes. "He instinctively understood that he had to think differently about the use of space, camera movement and lighting," Kovacs says. "There are many scenes where we just let the actors move through the space and keep the camera relatively quiet. The coverage was very different than what Troy originally planned. We didn't punch in on a lot of big close-ups."

Kovacs had his first camera assistant, Tony Nagy, work with Panavision to test and compare the anamorphic lenses on his rental list and make certain they all matched in terms of color-rendering and other image-capture characteristics. But just a few days before the camera truck was ready to load and roll to the first location, the filmmakers' desire to shoot widescreen still hadn't been approved by the studio.

"There are still myths about costs," notes Kovacs, "but the reality is that although anamorphic lenses rent for a nominally higher price, that's a small part of the budget. Some people still think it takes more light to shoot in anamorphic; that perception goes back to the original CinemaScope lenses, which created about a two-stop light loss, and in those days the color negative film had an exposure index of 25 or maybe 50. Today we're shooting with the Kodak Vision 500-speed film and incredible lenses."

Finally, at the last possible moment, producer Tadross came through.

Miller brought a young production designer named Mayne Schuyler Berke, who had a background in theater and TV, onto the project. Berke impressed Kovacs with his visual acuity. Kovacs had the luxury of approximately two months of prep with Berke and Miller, and he says that investment paid big dividends in the design of film-friendly sets and locations.

The cast and crew opened production by shooting establishing scenes in Truckee and the Donner Pass for three weeks. During that time, Kovacs recalls, there were about three and a half days of sunlight and many unexpected overcast days. He had a second unit headed by cinematographer Clyde Smith at those locations for about 40 days. Later, Miller and Kovacs brought the first unit back to Truckee to wrap up scenes with actors.

The Long Beach hangar is dome-shaped, which meant it was impossible to hang lights from the ceiling because it couldn't hold the weight. Kovacs had to dream up another way to light the giant set. In addition to the five house exteriors and street, there were tall pine trees and artificial snow piled 3 to 4 feet high. The set was ringed with white muslin that was visible at sky level behind the trees. Kovacs lit the muslin to emulate a gray, overcast sky; there was no money for sky replacement, so he was careful to avoid lights and other objects at the top frameline.

Kovacs' solution to the lighting dilemma was novel. "We built two bridge-like structures at 45-degree angles to the set," he says. "They were three stories high. We had every type of lamp we needed on the bridges, along with two 20-by-120-foot diffusion frames, which were used to soften the light depending on the scene and time of day."

The TransLites were 125 feet down the street, so there were daylight scenes where Kovacs lit huge areas that had to be properly balanced. At night, simulated moonlight, street lamps and pools of warm light from windows did the job. "When we switched from shooting a day to a night scene, the grips had it rigged so that frames with blue gels came down in front of the lamps while we reduced the intensity of light. We also programmed the computer to account for angles, colors and intensity of other light sources, including street and house lights and holiday decorations."

Kovacs initially estimated that it would take as long as two hours to make a day-to-night (or vice versa) lighting change on the big set. By the end of the shoot, however, it was taking no longer than 20 minutes.

With the faster films and lenses, Kovacs says he can also use smaller lights with combinations of diffusion and color gels to create visual nuances. "Anyone can learn how to record perfectly exposed pictures," he told Miller. "The art is in the way you control light. Light can be tactile and affect how the audience feels the coldness and experiences the darkness. The more freedom we have in controlling light, the more creative we can get."

The fact that they were shooting in the anamorphic format energized the collaborative process. "Troy and I discussed the aesthetics and the dos and don'ts," says Kovacs. "One of the advantages of shooting interiors in Charlie's house [another series of sets] is that you don't see the floor or ceiling, so you can lay dolly tracks and hang lights. We designed sets with removable walls. In a very small room, we were able to remove a wall and get farther back with the camera without using an unnaturally wide-angle lens. On the other hand, we had to be careful so that the camera always felt like it was in the same room as the characters. You have to watch the angles so they seem realistic.

"You also have to think about composition on a conscientious level, not only how you balance a shot, but also how every shot flows into the next one," he continues. "The fact that the snowman is taller than Charlie automatically created empty space, so we had to decide how to use it. There is always a compositional element you can use in that part of the frame — an object in the house or yard, or something down the road."

The company converted an interior set left over from *Batman & Robin* into a secret pond where Charlie goes to remember times when he used to play hockey with his dad. Kovacs notes that since it was right next to the street sets, virtually no time was lost making moves. That's important when your lead actor is a juvenile with limited hours.

"I gave Mayne Berke the same advice I have for all production designers on anamorphic films: make the sets about 25 percent larger than reality," Kovacs says. "Usually their first reaction is reluctance. I have to convince them that the audience won't notice if it doesn't mirror reality, and it will give us room to shoot from more interesting angles. I also tell them not to worry about the ceiling or floor — that makes the prop guys happy! They don't have to worry about rolling up carpets, and it's a lot easier to put clear marks on the floor that doesn't get in the shot. It's also great for the sound man because he can come in close to the actors with the boom."

How do you make a story like *Jack Frost* magical and believable at the same time?

Kovacs doesn't have a pat answer. On *Jack Frost,* he tried to show the audience Charlie's point of view without taking the camera down to the child's level. "I wanted it to work emotionally from his point of view, the way he sees the snowman, including when he's talking to him," Kovacs says. "The audience isn't going to buy the idea that the snowman is real if you treat that issue too seriously. You run the risk of it becoming laughable. But in the heat of the emotions, you can believe that the spirit of his father has returned to complete some unfinished business."

Kovacs cites a pivotal scene where Charlie is building the snowman on a cold, dark night. "Troy [Miller] played beautiful, sweet-sounding music before we shot that scene," he recalls. "That was important because it helped to define our lighting. We had to decide how dark and threatening to make the night. And how romantic are the Christmas lights compared to the previous year, when Charlie's dad was alive?" (Don't try finding the answers to those questions in a film-school textbook. Kovacs says the answers only live in your heart and in your visual memory.)

In the scene, Charlie builds a new snowman, and after that he's in his bedroom, looking at it through a window, when he thinks he sees it move. Charlie gets closer to the window, and then he gets scared when it moves again. He climbs into his bed and hides under the covers. But soon he's peering out the window again. The camera moves to the window and passes through it, leading to a Steadicam shot swirling faster and faster around the snowman. Suddenly, the camera stops. Everything is quiet. The snowman blinks, moves an eye, adjusts its mouth and speaks with Keaton's voice.

"It's truly a magical moment," Kovacs observes. He remembers feeling a chill when he saw that shot in dailies. "The widescreen format made it seem larger than life, but it was everything working together — the colors, lighting, mood and the way the music prepared us to shoot the scene."

Kovacs considered shooting *Jack Frost* at a stop of T5.6, but he decided that T4 provided crisp depth of field with the 500-speed film. Blue gels knocked the light level down to T2.8 at night, but that wasn't a problem because the filmmakers felt there should be less depth of field at night.

The bridge that held the overhead lamps was slightly bent in the middle, and that gave Kovacs the ability to create three-quarter soft backlight. The lamps were staggered, with a big lamp placed above a smaller one. Right next to that alignment was a small lamp placed above a bigger one, with black flags aligned to erase any spill light. The second bridge was interlocked with the first one by catwalks and other rigging that kept it stable. "The bridges carried a tremendous amount of weight," says Kovacs. "The catwalks enabled the grips to move quickly when we re-rigged from day to night and night to day. That basically involved dropping blue gels and diffusion in front of the lamps to alter the color and character of light. Every light was programmed through the dimmer board. We could push some buttons and alter the color and intensity of the light for the next shot."

Kovacs says his main objective was lighting the sets so they looked real, but that was sometimes tempered by instinct. "When I'm outside at night and the moon is visible, I never see blue light; it's more of a cool gray. But you have to rely on your instincts, and in some scenes we wanted the quality of light to be magical rather than realistic, so the hue is blue instead of gray."

Kovacs says the action or drama in the scene always dictated the quality and level of light on screen. "In one scene we wanted enough light on one side of Charlie's face for the audience to see his tears. Deep shadows mask the other side of his face. I've always remembered a lesson my teacher in film school, George Illes, taught me. He said, 'You always have to light the darkness; otherwise there is nothing but black.'"

Two types of artificial snow were used on the show, plastic and a combination of wood chips and crushed ice. Kovacs estimates that the studio ran through some 600 tons of ice.

"You have to be careful lighting snow because it's much more reflective than a grass yard or an asphalt road," he says. "We were dealing with huge, snow-flocked trees, snow on the ground and snow banks made from blocks of Styrofoam. They began dressing the set with snow and ice at 4 a.m. They were amazingly artistic in making it look real; it gathered and clung to the corners of buildings and covered the ground."

Kovacs lit day exteriors with soft light, emulating overcast days. He never created direct sunlight. A single 20K wouldn't have been sufficient, he explains, because of the huge area that had to be covered, and two or three big units would have created two or three shadows of the snowman and other characters.

Kovacs used Kodak Vision 500T 5279 for day and night interiors and exteriors. He likes the way it renders "vividly saturated primary colors. The Christmas lights play off Charlie's skin tones with soft pastels, and we have sparkling white snow and dark black shadows in scenes with a rich spectrum of contrast and colors."

Kovacs worked closely with John Bickford at Technicolor Labs, continuing a long-term relationship that is important to the cinematographer. "He knows my tastes and understands that I like to lock in on a one-light print very early. I didn't want him to correct from shot to shot, or even scene to scene. I always know exactly where I am with interior lighting because I'm controlling all sources."

Kovacs used black flags to create negative fill that soaked up ambient light leaking into interior and exterior scenes. It was like painting with a subtle brush.

"I love very rich, saturated prints with blacks that are really black," he says. "The compliment you want to hear from John Bickford is that your dailies look like ENR prints. I learned a long time ago that what you put into the negative is what you get back."

Despite the fact that *Jack Frost* was a relatively low-budget film, Kovacs says the filmmakers "had all the toys we needed: a Technocrane with a 30-foot extension and a portable Lenny minicrane from Chapman. The Lenny wasn't as flexible as the Technocrane, but it was light enough to dolly on soft snow and probed deep into scenes with a 38-foot-long extension.

" When you're working on uneven, soft surfaces like snow in the mountains at 7,000- and 8,000-foot elevations, you can't build a dolly track, no matter how hard you try. It sinks into the snow and makes everyone miserable, including the grips and your crew. I had great

Steadicam operator, Neil Norton, who Vilmos [Zsigmond, ASC] and Dick Donner discovered on *Maverick.* He worked with me on *Free Willy 2, Copycat* and *My Best Friend's Wedding.* He was also my A-camera operator."

Kovacs estimates that he shot 60 percent of *Jack Frost* with a Steadicam, in part because it was difficult to do conventional tracking on a dolly in the soft snow. He also wanted to break up the stillness occasionally with an interestingly choreographed camera move.

He had two camera operators, Norton and Don Thorin Jr., working most of the time. His other assistants were Steve Aredas, Trevor Loomis, Rodney Sandoval and Chad Rivetti. The two primary cameras were provided by Panaflex. Kovacs also used an Arriflex 435 camera, mainly for slow-motion shots.

Greg Smith was the camera operator on the second crew, and Chris Squires handled Steadicam shots. Tom Ryan and Rob Blake were the assistant cameramen.

Jack Frost has an interesting end-game scene guaranteed to tug at your heart. All winters come to an end, and this one is no exception. Spring arrives, and the snowman begins melting. Charlie tries to save him by bringing him to a mountain cabin at a higher elevation.

How does it end? There is only one way to find out: take a couple of 10-year-olds to the movie and see for yourself.

First published in *International Photographer*, December 1998.

PHOTO: SUZANNE HANOVER

Kovacs takes a light reading at an exterior location for *Jack Frost* (1998).

Kovacs on location with director Dennis Hopper during production of *Easy Rider* (1969).

9

Kovacs and Pearl Revisit the Past, Focus on the Future

by

Bob Fisher

The headline on a recent front-page article in the *Los Angeles Times* read "New Digital Cameras Poised to Jolt World of Filmmaking." The story focused on Mike Figgis, the director who crafted *Leaving Las Vegas.* Figgis was shooting *Timecode 2000* for Sony Pictures with four digital-video cameras. The reporter lumped *Timecode 2000* in with *The Blair Witch Project* and concluded: "Digital video makes filmmakers more mobile, better able to shoot scenes without cocooning themselves in studios or at on-site locations, and freer to move through the bustle of real city streets, even interacting with real people."

Nice research. The reporter only missed the mark by 30 years. Remember *Easy Rider*? Apparently, he didn't. Dennis Hopper and Peter Fonda, aided and abetted by Jack Nicholson, took the audience on a visceral ride through the dark side of America in 1969. They covered some 3,000 miles in 12 weeks, shooting with one camera, a few lenses and minimalist lighting. Leonard Maltin called *Easy Rider* a landmark film that began a small-picture revolution. It also changed the art of moviemaking.

The cinematographer was Laszlo Kovacs. There was no ASC (American Society of Cinematographers) after Kovacs' name in those days — he couldn't even get into the camera guild. Kovacs was a political refugee who had fled Hungary after the Russian army crushed an attempt to overthrow the Communist regime in Budapest in 1956. Kovacs was in his final year of film school when the revolt spilled into the streets. Kovacs and another student, Vilmos Zsigmond, filmed the brutal conflicts between civilians and tanks. "We hid the camera in a shopping bag," Kovacs says, "because if we got caught we could have been shot. One of us was the lookout while the other one was shooting."

When the revolt failed, Kovacs and Zsigmond made a perilous dash for the border, hauling some 30,000 feet of film in potato bags, because they thought the world should see the truth. After landing in America, Kovacs spent most of the next 10 years working at odd jobs, ranging from tapping maple syrup from trees to processing newsreels for a TV station. He mainly shot film on weekends. Kovacs was discovered by Dick Rush, a young director who specialized in making films that usually played as the second feature in drive-ins.

"Dennis Hopper saw *Psych-Out*, a very-low-budget film I shot for Dick, and asked if I was interested in *Easy Rider*," Kovacs says. "I turned him down because I'd had my fill of motorcycle films. He wanted a meeting anyhow, and I agreed. It was the best decision I ever made. He acted out the script, and I realized it was a great story about America. The next day, several of us drove to New Orleans, stopping to scout locations along the way."

Kovacs says that *Easy Rider* was an exercise in minimalist filmmaking. "We had the motorcycles in one truck and all the camera and lighting gear in another. There was no room for a dolly. My camera car was a Chevy convertible with a plywood platform. The film looks spontaneous, but don't let that fool you. We rehearsed and staged every scene, and I lit to establish the mood and setting."

Easy Rider earned kudos at Cannes and was a revelation at the box office. Kovacs says it was the film that made him believe he had a future in Hollywood. He went on to shoot some 60 narrative films, including *Five Easy Pieces; The King of Marvin Gardens; The Last Movie; Paper Moon; Shampoo; New York, New York; Ghostbusters; Mask; Copycat,* and *My Best Friend's Wedding.*

Cut to Daniel Pearl, who shot *The Texas Chainsaw Massacre*, another seminal film that altered the art of filmmaking, 25 years ago. Pearl was a 23-year-old graduate of the University of Texas when Tobe Hooper asked him to shoot his film. "I had just earned a graduate degree in filmmaking so I could teach," says the New Jersey native, "because I was told it was impossible for an outsider like me to break into the film industry. We made this film for about $80,000 with a 16mm camera, which I frequently handheld, and 25-speed color positive film."

The Texas Chainsaw Massacre earned rave reviews at Cannes and was a runaway hit at the box office. A critic called it a near-perfect horror film that gave movie fans a new experience. *Chainsaw* has the feel of a cinéma vérité documentary. "There were no portable 35mm cameras available to us," Pearl says. "We shot in 16mm because of the tension you can get with a handheld camera. I shot with an Éclair NPR camera, and we used movement and composition to pull the audience into the story from the subject's viewpoint. The 16mm color negative available at that time was very grainy. I used Ektachrome ECO film, which was virtually grainless, because it didn't draw attention to the photography. My guess is that the light we needed for exposing images was about 20 times more intense than what we'd need today."

After *Chainsaw*, Pearl shot about a dozen low-budget features, all in the horror genre. In 1982 a young director named Russell Mulcahey asked if he was interested in working on some promos for record companies. Pearl thought it would be fun and a good way to fill the time between narrative films. He has since compiled some 800 music-video and TV-commercial credits, earning countless awards. *Fortune* magazine called Pearl one of the most influential people in the music-video industry.

On the respective 30th and 25th anniversaries of their landmark films, we asked Kovacs and Pearl to reflect on the evolving role of the cinematographer.

Kovacs had just wrapped *Return to Me*, a character-driven film made on a $20 million budget with first-time director Bonnie Hunt. He has been on the festival circuit, accompanying a restored print of *Easy Rider* and talking with young would-be filmmakers. "I'm almost embarrassed by the response to *Easy Rider*," says Kovacs. "Around 400 people came to see it at a festival in Flagstaff, and there were even more in Dallas. One documentary filmmaker rode in on a Harley, leading around 40 bikers. He said when he saw *Easy Rider* it became his dream to own a Harley."

Kovacs says most people assume he shot *Easy Rider* from the hip because the film exudes a feeling of freedom. He says every shot was lit to create a visual texture. "Many of the young people I've met at festivals tell me they're using digital cameras because it's cheap and they can reuse the tape. That's okay, as long as they understand that video and film don't see light the same way. Others say they like digital cameras because they don't have to light; they just push a gain-control button. I tried to tell them that light is the medium we use to create moods and a sense of time and place. If you aren't lighting, you're just recording images. It's not the same art."

We caught Pearl during a quick stopover in Los Angeles. He had been in Hong Kong, Japan and Brazil, shooting for the umpteenth time with Mariah Carey, and was on his way to New York to shoot another commercial.

Pearl recalls that he had only been out of school for a few weeks and had just a few local and regional commercial credits when Hooper said he wanted a Texan to shoot *The Texas Chainsaw Massacre*. Pearl was actually a New Jersey native, but was considered a transplant Texan because he'd been living there for almost eight years.

"I had no idea that we were going to shoot a cult film that would endure for 25 years," he says, "but I knew it was a great opportunity when I read the screenplay. I was afraid that Tobe would decide to get Laszlo Kovacs or Vilmos Zsigmond or someone like that, so I called him right away and asked when we were going to start shooting. He said he had one investor who'd put up $70,000 and he needed $10,000 more. I found the remaining $10,000 in order to get it under way. I didn't want to lose the project."

We asked Kovacs to speculate on what made *Easy Rider* so popular with the public.

"The movie has a spirit that people like. My favorite scene is the last campfire before Jack [Nicholson] gets killed. It features incredible writing by Terry Southern, and Jack gave a superb performance. The [important] thing is that the audience liked these long-haired hippies. I still remember Jack's line, 'You know, this used to be a helluva good country,' and Dennis' response about not even being able to get a haircut. When they're killed, it shocks the audience. I knew something important was happening, and I didn't want to mess it up. It makes me feel really good when people come out of festival screenings today and ask the same questions I heard thirty years ago."

Pearl remembers that he and Hooper talked about *Easy Rider*, and George Romero's *Night of the Living Dead* and *The Legend of Boggy Creek* before shooting *Chainsaw*. "Those films were our inspiration, especially *Easy Rider*. It proved that you could make a good film outside of the Hollywood system.

"Tobe was a cinematographer prior to becoming a director, so he had a very strong visual sense. We thought out every shot; we weren't just running around with a camera. We planned for it to be terrifying. Tobe and I had an organic approach to shooting. After a week of photography, the producers shut us down for five days and told Tobe he had to write a shot list. But it was a placebo.

"Two days later we were shooting an exterior scene with an actress on a swing. We finished the shot, and I turned to Tobe and said I had an idea. We had a flatbed dolly, and I said if I could get behind the swing with a camera, we could lay track all the way up to the front steps and follow the girl when she got up and walked toward the house. I wanted to lie down on the dolly and hold the camera off the edge to get a very low angle. It's terrifying, because the audience is walking with her and they know what's in the house."

Pearl recalls Hooper telling the producer that he could fire them, but he couldn't stop them from making that shot. Pearl had an 8mm lens on the camera. As the actress got up and walked toward the house, he dollied under the swing. She stayed a constant size, but the house loomed larger and larger, right up to the top of the frame. "Many years later, Steven Spielberg asked me about that shot," Pearl says.

"*Chainsaw* was 25 years ago, and I feel like I've been constantly racing to keep up with the audience. They've become much more sophisticated and their tastes have broadened. They'll accept a *Blair Witch Project* as long as it has artistic integrity. It can be gritty as long as it's the right look for the story. I agree with Laszlo that people who think you can push a button instead of lighting will have short careers."

We asked Kovacs and Pearl about the convergence of digital postproduction and film.

"The role of the cinematographer has been changing," says Kovacs. "We're doing more of our work in post, but that doesn't change the aesthetics. I shot a film a couple of years ago, *Multiplicity*, in which Michael Keaton played four roles, and he was composited into every scene interacting with himself. That affected how we lit and staged almost every scene. Some people will try to reinterpret the cinematographer's work in digital post; ad agencies do it with commercials all the time. But [good cinematography] still takes an eye and a sense of what the story is about."

Pearl expects more of an evolution than a revolution. He cautions that over-reliance on CGI and other image manipulation can result in a sterile look. "Sometimes I look at a CG shot and could swear that it's real," he says. "Other times, the spontaneity is missing. You can do anything in telecine, and that can be a fantastic tool, but unless you retain the integrity of the artistic idea you strip away the emotions. I think that when the novelty wears off, there will be a push to do as much as possible in original photography and then involve the cinematographer in the digital suite."

Pearl continues, "It all starts with lighting — that's where we start to shape the look and emotions. It's not just about having enough light to shoot; it's about how we manipulate emotions and focus the attention of the audience with light. We can make them look any place in the frame and control what they see and don't see. Some of the scariest stuff in *Chainsaw* is when Leatherface emerges out of the shadows, and before you know it he's in the middle of the frame. We did that with a combination of light and composition — we directed the eye to one side of the frame while he entered from the other side. By the time you notice him, he's on top of his prey. It makes the audience jump out of their seats every time.

"You need a vision going into a film," he adds. "The digital tools in post are great, but you can't get that type of impact in post."

First published in *In the Industry*, January 2000.

PHOTO: CHRIS HELECERMANAS-BENGE

First-time director Bonnie Hunt during filming of *Return to Me* (2000).

10

Laszlo Kovacs Talks About a Love Story

by

Bob Fisher

In 1968 Laszlo Kovacs joined first-time director Dennis Hopper on a trek through the Southwestern United States to make *Easy Rider.* It was a film that sparked a new way of thinking about where and how movies could and should be made.

Thirty-one years later Kovacs was working with another first-time director, Bonnie Hunt, only this time he was shooting a romantic comedy on location in Chicago. The film, *Return to Me,* was co-written by Hunt and Don Lake. (Hunt also plays an important supporting role in the film.)

The film opens at an elegant, black-tie charity ball, where Elizabeth Rueland's (Joely Richardson) dream is about to blossom. The successful event will assure that a habitat she has designed for a gorilla at the Chicago Zoo will be built. The film then cuts away to a restaurant run by Marty O'Reilly (Carroll O'Connor) and his friend, Angelo (Robert Loggia). The regulars include O'Reilly's granddaughter Grace (Minnie Driver). Dialogue reveals that Grace is in desperate need of a heart transplant. On that cue, the story cuts back to the fundraiser. Elizabeth and her husband Bob (David Duchovny) drive home in separate cars, and she is killed in an auto accident. When Elizabeth dies, Grace gets her heart and a new outlook on life. About a year later, Grace and Bob's lives intersect, and they fall in love.

"This film was organically designed for Chicago," Kovacs says. "Bonnie lived in Chicago, where she was involved with the Second City comedy troupe for a long time. Every part of this story draws on her memories of those times. [The primary location was] a neighborhood restaurant where Bonnie had sat in the same corner booth with her boyfriend and future husband practically every night for a year."

Return to Me was produced and distributed by MGM on a comparatively sparse $20 million budget. Producer Jennie Lew Tugent knew Kovacs from several other films, including *Radio Flyer* and *Free Willy2,* and she introduced him to Hunt. Kovacs had recently shot *My Best Friend's Wedding* in the Windy City, so he already knew the electrical crew and grips.

MGM asked him to assemble an all-Chicago camera crew, so Kovacs reached out to George Kohut, who had done some B-camera work for him on *My Best Friend's Wedding.* His first assistant was Peter Kuttner, backed by Jennifer Desplinter-Anderson, and his loader was Kristine Scott Schultz.

The decision to shoot *Return to Me* in the 1.85:1 Academy format was made before Kovacs came on the scene, but he notes that the format suited the film's small practical locations. It also allowed him to compose full-figure shots with wide-angle lenses without a hint of distortion.

"Bonnie kept reminding us this was her first movie as a director, but she had more knowledge about filmmaking than she let anybody believe," Kovacs observes. "I discovered that right away. We shot our opening scene in a beautiful, old ballroom, and she was able to communicate exactly what she wanted. She didn't say, 'I want the camera put here or there, and then we're going to follow that actor,' but she always told me the most important things she wanted from the scene. I knew the emotional highs and lows. The actors respected and loved her because she was doing the right thing for them. She and I discussed blocking and setting up shots; I offered suggestions for making shots more fluid, and she caught on quickly."

The opening ballroom scene posed a contrast to the rest of the picture because its setting was so opulent. Kovacs was very specific about the placement of each light and used a laser pointer to pinpoint the location for each lamp. He notes that if a light is misaligned by only a few feet in either direction, it can change the mood of a scene. "It was a huge room, and it had a balcony that was very useful," he recalls. "We used it almost like a catwalk and placed some lights on it." There were a dozen 10Ks and at least as many 4Ks overhead, and there were also a number of 4Ks punching through 6'x6' and 8'x8' panels of diffusion on the floor.

"We had as many as 500 people seated in groups of 10 at big tables. The scene opens up with Bob Rueland [Duchovny] and his wife projecting slides about the habitat in the zoo. The screen reflected bounce light and became a primary light source. She was standing at a little podium, and there was a spotlight on her. We had different-sized shots, from extreme wide angles to close-ups and medium shots. I used two cameras, so we got a wide shot and a single on her at the same time. Bonnie kept claiming that she didn't know a lot about making movies, but I never took her seriously. I could see that she was always thinking about the visual sequences. That made it much easier to communicate."

During preproduction, Hunt told Kovacs about the characters and her old neighborhood, and showed him photographs of courtyards, streets and the restaurant that she wanted to use as the main location. "The restaurant looked awfully small, and there were narrow spaces between tables," he remembers. "It looked like you could almost touch the ceiling — there was about a foot and a half of clearance! I tried to tell her we'd have at least a dozen people besides the actors on the set, so we'd be in very tight space. I could see from her expression that she wasn't happy at the thought of not shooting there. She explained why it was important for her to shoot at that particular restaurant.

"I was horrified when I actually saw the place for the first time, because there was no room for any film equipment," he continues. "Bonnie finally agreed, after a lot of pain, to let us shoot in the booth next to [her old one] so that we could get some shots from different angles."

The show's gaffer and grip quickly discovered that there were tiles covering a false ceiling in the restaurant, and above the false ceiling was about four feet of crawl space. That space allowed Kovacs to use a combination of backlight, edgelight and crosslight; the audience always sees three walls, he explains, but he and Hunt staged angles and composition so there was always some sidelight and crosslight creating a sense of depth. "Above the false ceiling were pipes for water and air-conditioning and electrical conduits, and we clamped lights on them," he explains. "That allowed us to create some separation between the actors and walls. There were no windows in the restaurant, so our light was basically motivated by practicals. I never lit day and night the same way, even if it was the same sources. I always tried to adapt it to the situation — I lit with more shadows in dramatic scenes and used softer, more romantic light at other times."

Kovacs notes that the restaurant was like a character in the film and had a lot of charm. "At times it was crowded, and during off hours there were only a few principal characters there. We made it darker when there were only a few people there, and when there were a lot of people it became a little more festive."

Hunt, coming from a TV background, was attuned to video-assist. Kovacs tried to help her maintain closer communication with the cast, particularly in the restaurant, by placing the monitor where she could communicate with the actors without shouting from a far corner of the room. He put the monitor in a booth or on a table close to the camera so Hunt could have eye contact with the actors.

"Bonnie would sometimes tell me to tighten up a shot, and I'd remind her very politely that it was going to look different on a big movie screen," he notes. "The truth is, it's hard to see anything on a 9-inch screen in a dark room. She would usually ask me to show her [the framing] both ways, and very often she didn't come in quite as tight as she originally intended.

"Another problem with video-assist is that there's usually an AD and producer standing there with the director. Filmmaking is a collaborative process, but you can't make decisions by committee. I notice how it affects the actors when there are three or four heads around a monitor talking for 30 to 40 seconds after the director says, 'Cut.' It can break their concentration. I try to watch for things like that and try to keep the mood on an even keel. This problem didn't arise too much with Bonnie, maybe because she's an actress."

Kovacs says that Hunt, the location manager and the assistant director were open to shooting exteriors at certain times of the day when the light was right for a scene. Sometimes they had to convince a property to allow them to shoot earlier or later than planned. "We had a wonderful AD, Artist Robinson, who was a close ally. He understood everything I was trying to do. He asked what time I wanted to shoot particular scenes and how long I needed. He would then go through that schedule with the actors and director. It wasn't always easy, because sometimes an actor would want an earlier or a later call for personal reasons; so Artist juggled and shuffled the schedule to give me what I needed. Sure, you can compromise and shoot flat-lit or with crosslighting, but I try not to settle for something I don't believe is good enough." Kovacs had a single afternoon to shoot exterior tests to find the middle of the scale on the printing lights.

On one big exterior at the zoo, Hunt wanted to make a 300'-long dolly shot with no people or animals in the scene. She couldn't explain how she was going to use that shot but insisted it was necessary, Kovacs says. The problem was that he wasn't carrying 300 feet of track, and the ground was sloping. The production considered hiring a Steadicam operator but decided that it would cost less to rent and build the track. "We never used a Steadicam," Kovacs says. "On walking-and-talking shots, we dollied in the old-fashioned, classical way."

For the film's interiors and night scenes, Kovacs used Kodak Vision 500T 5279, and for day exteriors he used Vision 200T 5274. "The fleshtones and colors in the new 200 film are very close to the old [Eastman EXR] 5293 film, which I liked, only with less grain."

Kovacs has been partial to Panavision since 1970, when Bob Gottshalk, the company's founder, brought one of the first PSR models to the location where he was shooting *Alex in Wonderland*. On *Return to Me* his lens package included a few primes and a 5:1 zoom.

For many years, Kovacs preferred zoom lenses; he shot most of *Easy Rider*, *Five Easy Pieces*, *The King of Marvin Gardens* and *Shampoo* with a 10:1 zoom. "I noticed that when Sony Pictures recently restored those films, it made scene-to-scene corrections very easy because everything was recorded through the same optical glass," he observes. "It's easier [to use them] today because modern zooms are a lot sharper with great optical quality. I shoot as much as I can with one zoom at variable focal lengths. I always keep a couple of primes standing by in case I get into a corner at a location and want a couple of extra feet.

"I don't like to carry a lot of toys or unnecessary equipment," he adds. "I didn't use any filtration on *Return to Me* because I wanted clear, sharp images."

For the first week to 10 days of the shoot, Astro Labs in Chicago processed the negative and provided film dailies. Kovacs was often viewing timed dailies by 7:30 the following morning. "That's when we had to establish the look," he says. "After [the first week] we shipped the negative to Deluxe in Los Angeles, where a local postproduction house transferred the film to high-definition video.

"The first day [of hi-def dailies] was just horrendous," he continues. "It looked awful — the image was washed out and lacked texture. We had shot an 18-percent gray scale card, correctly lit and exposed, before every scene, and even the card looked like a very light gray. There was no color and no blacks. I told Bonnie, 'I'm not coming to see these dailies because they're not representative of our work, and they'll give you the wrong idea.' I was also worried about scene-to-scene matching. Eventually I set up a system with Deluxe: I selected the two most important shots each day, and they put them on a Hazeltine and told me what I needed to know about my printing lights."

MGM also previewed *Return to Me* for audiences in hi-def, claiming that it saved $200,000 and more closely resembled the final film than a workprint would. They showed Kovacs a rough cut on a small monitor and gave him about three hours to do some quick color corrections. He says that the colorist must have worked through the night to make the changes he suggested. "When I saw it projected on a big screen at the studio the next day, it looked very good — or at least as good as hi-def is going to look on a big screen," Kovacs says. "It was kind of flat and lacked rich blacks and saturated color. It's TV, not film.

"You can really notice the difference when you have a beautifully backlit scene with luminescent colors, and a character's hair is supposed to be sparkling with highlights. On hi-def, everything looks flat, which creates a different mood. One of a cinematographer's major contributions is that he creates images that help the audience sense moods and feelings. You don't choose to backlight a scene because you think it's pretty; you do it because you're listening to the director, watching the actors and helping them tell their story."

Kovacs credits a talented wardrobe designer, Lis Bothwell, with understanding the importance of choosing the right fabrics and colors for the actors, particularly in the film's opening scene at the charity ball. "She was very concerned about white because someone on another picture had told her to never bring white on his set," he says. "She asked me what I wanted her so do about the men's shirts — did I want her to tech them down? Between actors and extras, we had 80 men in that sequence! I told her not to worry. I felt differently years ago, because the older films couldn't handle whites without blowing out. I tended to use fog and other filters and diffusion in those days. But the Kodak Vision films have so much more latitude today. I love white now, because it's so pure and gives you a reference for black.

"Lis always showed me samples of fabrics and asked about colors and textures. She also understood how costumes have to work with locations. I think the use of colors by the production and costume designers was very tasteful and important in this film."

Kovacs explains that costumes and colors make statements to the audience about the personality of the characters, but that's only part of it. "You can use color like composition to draw attention to certain parts of the frame. Say, for example, that you're staging a scene and the main characters are in the foreground. You may not want the audience's eyes to stray to a character in the dark background just because he happens to be wearing a white shirt. So you would want that person to be in a more subdued costume. This is something cinematographers have to be very conscious of, because so many production and costume designers and directors are coming from music videos, commercials and TV, where they don't have to think about the same considerations."

Kovacs says there are at least two types of technical knowledge essential for every cinematographer. One is an understanding of how different films will react in any situation, and the other is an understanding of the effects of different lenses. He says he begins every day by walking up to the camera, touching the magazine and saying, "Good morning."

He avoided intricate camera moves on *Return to Me* "because it didn't lend itself to the story. We composed a lot of shots four or five people sitting around a table, shooting the breeze." Kovacs says he worked hard with Hunt on composition. If there were four or five people in a scene but only two mattered, then staging, composition and how the camera would pan were all important decisions, along with the lighting and continuity. Hunt gave him a lot of freedom, but Kovacs was also sensitive to her ideas and showed her the setups.

"We want the audience to feel like they're watching real people in a real situation," he says. "But there is no such thing as a simple shot, and the crew did a great job. They had to be aware of every nuance with the actors and everything else in the frame. They had to be sensitive to what was coming into the frame, what was leaving it, and how that affected the scene. George Kohut was an extra set of eyes on composition and lighting; I counted on him to tell me if someone had missed a mark. Sometimes an accident like that can work for you, but I want to make that decision and not be surprised."

After Grace flees Chicago following an altercation with Bob, the lovers are reunited in Rome. Thanks to one of Kovacs' Italian colleagues, he had a top-notch crew at his disposal there. "I called Vittorio Storaro [ASC, AIC], and he happened to be on hiatus," Kovacs recalls. "I gave him the dates, and he said he'd make sure his camera, electrical and grip crews were available. I took my light meter, and that was all I needed.

"Bonnie had worked in Rome on a film called *Only You* with [director] Norman Jewison and [director of photography] Sven Nykvist [ASC], so she had some ideas about romantic locations that would tell the audience we were in Rome. She selected a beautiful, old church with a long oval shape, which is where she wanted the reunion to take place. It's an obvious landmark, maybe not like the Trevi Fountain, but it looks Roman."

They allotted three days for scouting locations. "On the first day, we pulled into a square and Bonnie just grabbed her heart — the monuments were covered in scaffolding! We found out that the government had decided to renovate all of them for the millennium, even St. Peter's. It was that way everywhere we went, except for the Parthenon. It didn't have scaffolding, but all the buildings behind it were covered. We were able to work around that.

"Night exteriors were difficult because the streets are so narrow that you can't even turn a truck around. Our generator would be on a truck three or four blocks away, connected by cable. It would have taken a day and a half to rig and a full night to shoot. I said to Bonnie, 'We need to talk. I know you want a romantic night scene at a sidewalk café…,' and she didn't let me finish. She said, 'This is *so* important. It's the end of the movie.' She was struggling with it like any director would have. She walked away, and after a couple of minutes she came back and agreed to shoot it in daylight."

Kovacs notes that the audience has to believe Bob is falling in love with Grace, and he lit Driver accordingly, keeping her mainly in three-quarter soft light. "I never actually met Minnie — I met the character she was playing from the first day on. Grace has a kind of a physical weakness about her when the film opens, but after the heart transplant she begins to take on a more assured look and attitude. Minnie couldn't always be in the same light, of course, but she had to look like the same character.

"There's a beautiful scene in which she's wearing a hat," Kovacs continues. "Hats give you an opportunity to create shadows and soft light on a face. Lis showed me the two hats she preferred, and the one I picked was kind of mid-toned and had some black motifs. It shaded Minnie's face and made her look very soft and beautiful. It's the moment that tells the audience Grace is in love, and we wanted her to shine."

Kovacs positioned the actress at an angle so the soft light he created would fall on her face, with a shadow from the brim of the hat partially obscuring one eye. There was no diffusion on the lens. "She was the same girl we met in the restaurant at the beginning of the film, but somehow she had become very elegant-looking and radiant. The lovers kiss, and everyone goes home happy."

First published in *ICG*, April 2000.

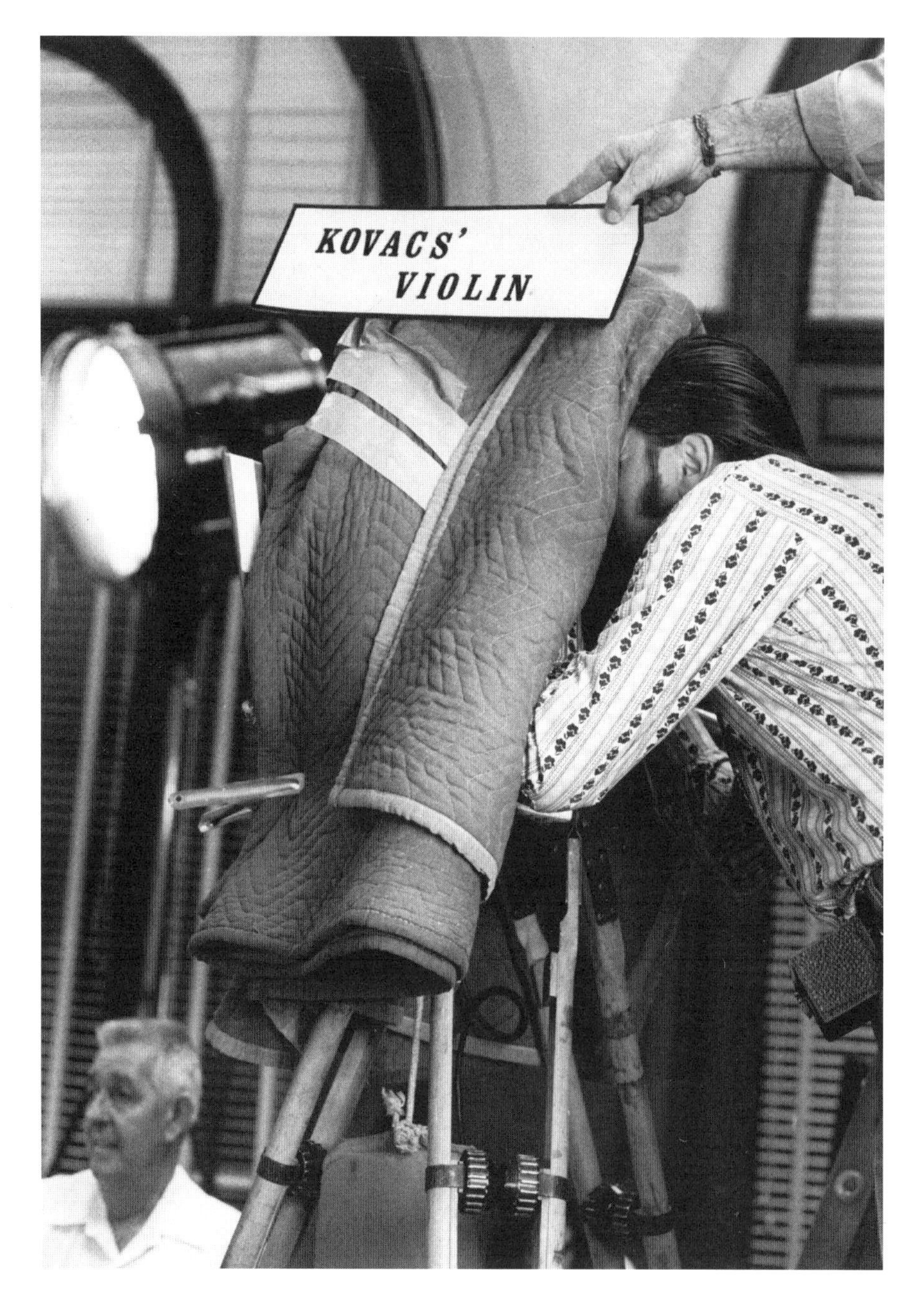

Kovacs says operating the camera is like playing a violin.

11

Kovacs' Violin: An Interview with Laszlo Kovacs, ASC

by

Ray Zone

In 1970, when Laszlo Kovacs was first informed that union guidelines required him to hire a camera operator, he said, "It's like my violin has been taken out of my hands. I give it to an operator, and I'm supposed to tell him how to play it." According to Kovacs' gaffer, Richard "Aggie" Aguilar, it was commonplace after that for the crew to affix a piece of tape to the camera that was labeled "Kovacs' Violin."

The following interview took place over two days at the American Society of Cinematographers (ASC) Clubhouse in November 2001. Because Kovacs has photographed more than 60 narrative feature films, it simply was not possible to discuss every one. Instead, the discussion is a career overview that highlights the way in which Kovacs' early career in Hollywood prepared him for the work that followed.

Ray Zone: You've photographed so many films, but a lot of your very early and more recent films seem to be rarely discussed.

Laszlo Kovacs: Nobody ever asks about them. I really fault the press, because I'm labeled 'the *Easy Rider* kid.' Out of 60-some movies, it seems like that's the only one I really did. But I read somewhere that somebody once told Orson Welles, 'Greta Garbo did two incredible movies.' Welles said, 'You only have to do one.'

I love your no-budget period. Did you assist Vilmos Zsigmond with the pictures he shot for Arch Hall Sr., films like *Spies a Go Go*?

Kovacs: Oh, yeah. That was us. We were the crew. Vilmos was shooting more stuff and he had his own Arri camera. I played a part in it as a village idiot. They blackened my teeth out, and I had a cowboy hat and a gun belt, with the gun hanging between my legs. Somebody told me that film is available on video somewhere!

You also worked with zero-budget horror director Al Adamson on *Blood of Dracula's Castle.*

Kovacs: Vilmos and I started that film together, but sometime early on Vilmos got a 'real' job. Working on that film was very funny. John Carradine got $700 in cash at the end of the day, and Adamson paid him with a lot of small bills. Carradine said, 'If I don't get my money, I'm not going to show up tomorrow.' That was the most important thing for him.

Al always paid with singles, and we wondered where all those singles came from. Al said, 'Before I come to work, I deliver newspapers. I like the money.'

At the end of the movie, we all got a check. The bank was City National Bank on Sunset Boulevard. Everybody jumped in his car, and there was a big race to the bank. The first eight or 10 checks would be paid and the rest of them would bounce!

You've had a very fruitful collaboration with Peter Bogdanovich, which overlapped your no-budget days with your low-budget days.

Kovacs: Yes. We shot *Targets* in 1966, immediately after some of those early biker movies like *The Savage Seven, Rebel Rouser* and *Hell's Angels on Wheels.* The production manager on those small movies came to me one day and said he had met this young director who was a film critic, and he was moving to California and was going to make his first film. He said, 'He wants somebody good and cheap.' I said, 'That's me.'

How did you light the drive-in *Targets?*

Kovacs: It was very tough, especially in those days, when we had slow film and small lighting units. We couldn't blind the actual audience at the drive-in, who were trying to watch a movie. We were shooting isolated over at the side, where Boris Karloff's car was parked next to the fence. We came in very early and did some of the arrival scenes at dusk, as well as the panic scenes where the audience realizes there's a killer and somebody is shooting at them. At the show's end, when everybody was leaving, we made it look like everybody was trying to get out. Old cars were being pushed out, creating some havoc.

The deal was that Peter was able to get financing for *Targets* from Roger Corman after he wrote the screenplay with his wife, Polly Platt. Corman gave him the money, which I think was $120,000, but he said, 'Boris Karloff owes me one week of work, and I'll deduct that.' That was something like $25,000. We had one week to use Karloff, so we were going crazy. It was very tough planning, even though the picture had the best schedule of any of my films up to that point — five weeks for shooting. Prior to that, the maximum I'd had was three or four weeks. We had to make those biker movies very fast.

Karloff was almost everywhere in *Targets.* He was in the beginning and the middle; he had a big scene in his hotel suite. And of course, he's at the drive-in for the big, climactic sequence. So we first shot him out completely.

It's a great example of how to make a fine film with limited resources.

Kovacs: It really is a good, terrifying movie. It wasn't based on a true story, but when we finished it a really scary thing happened at the University of Texas in Austin. Some young boy went up a tower at the university and started shooting people, and he killed about 14 of them. He drove a white Mustang convertible. Our hero in *Targets* also drove a white Mustang convertible. He left it at the drive-in in the closing shot.

We climbed up on top of the screen and shot the whole drive-in. A single white Mustang was left among all the garbage, and you hear the wind blowing and the sound of all the cars. It was very bizarre when that young man did something similar in Texas shortly after the film was completed. A similar incident also happened down by the San Diego Freeway, by the oil tanks. Every time I drive by there, I look up at those tanks.

Targets was also very interesting because we were filming without a permit. In the film, there's a guy aiming a telescopic rifle at the cars. We worked out a wonderful system for shooting that. We planted our cars at the drive-in with the passengers that were to be hit. At the briefing, we talked about my locking on the camera with crosshairs, with a long lens. I couldn't give the actors a signal because if I breathed, the camera moved; it's very sensitive with a long lens. So Peter got on a walkie-talkie, and he just said, 'Bang.' That was the actors' cue. We did all the sequences that way.

When we were planning the film, Corman told Bogdanovich, 'Of course, Peter, there are no opticals, none whatsoever, not even dissolves — only straight cuts.' But with that long lens, we needed to optically put the crosshair in a circle, like in a gun sight. I remember Peter calling me to the lab and saying, 'We need to time these opticals.' I said, 'What?!' And he said, 'Shhhh! It's the gun sight. I ordered it at the lab and charged it to Roger's other movies.' Roger never found out, but if he had, he probably would have laughed and let it go. Peter was very clever.

You filmed *Targets* right when you were going from your no-budget period into the low-budget period.

Kovacs: It was the first script given to me that was serious. It wasn't like those action/exploitation scripts with a bike gang coming to town and terrorizing people, getting drunk and driving away; that was basically the recipe for those biker movies. *Targets* was very substantial, a very dramatic story. It was a first for me.

At that time, were you still operating the camera yourself?

Kovacs: Absolutely. It was still the good old days. It was such a joy using my own camera! That was absolute satisfaction. During the take I could watch the image and control the camera moves. Many times, I had to do zoom and focus myself. I wouldn't even trust the assistant. In those days, the assistant wasn't as sophisticated with handling zoom and focus and judging the distance. It was an exciting time because it was me, my camera and the director; it was like complete authorship. I had heard that on big-time productions they were using operators, first assistants, second assistants and so forth, but at that point I couldn't bother with it. I felt it was so far in the future I didn't have to worry about it.

You were using an Arri camera, sometimes blimped for sync sound?

Kovacs: Yes, I always had an Arri II C with a zoom lens and three prime lenses on a turret. We usually had 28mm, 50mm and 75mm lenses with us. Whenever we shot MOS, we took the camera out of the blimp and put it on a regular tripod with a zoom lens. When we needed to do sound, we quickly put the camera back into the blimp. In those days we didn't have a proper hood to cover the lens from the sun, so we put a pad around it. I was operating by setting up the shot and executing the shot. I was making all those quick decisions when the actors started improvising. It was a discipline to respect the actor's art and not interrupt.

I still feel that way. I don't care how professional the actor is, it always makes you nervous to know that the glass is right there, looking at you. Very early on I discovered that I had to support actors and dissolve that kind of fear. So I did whatever it took, either a light joke or a distraction, so they wouldn't take the camera so seriously. But in the corner of their eyes, they always knew I was there.

Sometimes that could be very good. Jack Nicholson, for example, knew the camera so well. The lens would create the space for the actors, and Jack knew exactly where that space was and very rarely asked about it. He always figured out an approximation of where to stand by noticing where the camera was, and he also figured out the staging and blocking for the rest of the actors. Of course, with a zoom lens you never know when the camera is going to punch in to a tight close-up!

Nicholson was always listening. You could plant him in the middle of 10,000 people in a wide shot, and your eye is always going to go to him because he knows how to show up in a crowd. He never had a problem with any actor who was blocking him. Even in a tight two-shot, over the shoulder, where the actor in the foreground can shift a little bit and block the actor behind him, Jack could sense where his space was. When he gets blocked, he just shifts a little in the other direction, which is always perfect. He's the perfect film actor.

Tell me about the filming of *Five Easy Pieces*.

Kovacs: I remember that we traveled from Los Angeles to Bakersfield and then up the coast, all the way into Canada, and back. You can't do that in five weeks! We prepared the picture very well, and on location we planned very carefully.

We were looking for something special for that very moving scene with Jack and his father, but we didn't know exactly what. There's kind of a long shot when we see Jack pushing his father in a wheelchair near the ocean in the evening. I saw a really incredible sunset with the contour of a hill running down in a nice, sloping curve to the right. We didn't want to see the ocean [in the frame], but it was a perfect shot. I said to Bob Rafelson, the director, 'How about we put Jack and the wheelchair in silhouette way over the top of the crest of this slope and just have him push it and walk.' Bob looked at it and said, 'Oh, yeah. You're right.' We all scrambled to set up the camera, and they got the wheelchair — there was no prop truck. Jack headed up there, and it became a perfect shot in the film.

We were going to shoot an intense, emotional scene between Jack and his father somewhere where it was very private. Jack was very nervous about doing it, and he just kept postponing the scene. Bob worked with him and told me, 'I'm not going to push him into it.' We let him play with it for a while.

Then we found a beautiful meadow with wet atmosphere and a wet ground. Bob said, 'This is it. Let's park the trucks on the road.' We didn't have permits or cops and firemen. We just traveled, and whenever we saw something better than the pre-selected location we used it. The meadow was one of those 'Oh my God, that looks great!' type of places. Bob told Jack that it was time to do the scene. Jack came up with another excuse not to do it, but finally he said, 'Okay, but I don't want anybody there.' That was fair enough.

So I was operating the camera and Bob was recording the sound; it was just the two of us. The scene was basically three or four shots, but the monologue Jack did was a medium close-up. I was looking through the camera at his face, and he built up and then broke down. He was so emotional, and it was so touching. It was such an incredible confession to his father.

After he finished, we cut to a close-up of his father, who was paralyzed. The man who played his father wasn't even an actor; he owned a gallery on La Cienega in Los Angeles. But he did the part so perfectly — his eyes never even blinked, they just kind of fluttered. He was not dead or alive. That was one of the really emotional experiences on the film. Basically, Jack's life was something like that.

Was that the last film you operated on?

Kovacs: Yes. I operated on *Five Easy Pieces* for all but the last three days, when we had to shoot in Los Angeles. When we got to L.A., everyone told me, 'Don't touch the camera! Don't even look through it!' I said, 'Come on.' It was around Christmas, so I had some time off and could look for an operator. But it was very difficult because I didn't know anybody. I had never used an operator, and I'd never been in contact with any major studio productions. I didn't know how to find a really good operator.

There isn't a hard line separating the duties of operator and director of photography, even nowadays. The jobs overlap. The camera operator is also a director of photography in a way, because he needs to understand a lot of things. He needs to understand the story, and it isn't easy to know the motivation of the scene. But he can learn it by listening to the discussion among the director, the cinematographer and the actors, and by watching. The operator needs to be talented and sharp, because we can't lose any valuable time communicating on the set. I say, 'Did you hear this? This is what we need to do. This is what's happening.' When I'm setting up the shot, the operator is right there. The process is almost like thinking out loud.

It's very important to engage every one of your collaborators. Everybody all the way down the line needs to understand why things are done a certain way. Now, I don't expect an electrician to understand the meaning of the scene and all the elements of the composition; he just has to be able to set a light exactly the way I want it. And he can, because he knows instinctively what a single lamp can record. It's extremely important that the camera operator has that understanding. He needs to know why we're doing things with the composition and watching the light values.

Sometime during rehearsal, the camera operator will say, 'There's a spot back there that's really bright,' or, 'It's something way back in the corner.' That's exactly what I want. I'm glad he notices these things and calls my attention to them. Sometimes he's right, and we'll quickly make adjustments. If I watch the scene through the camera, I notice those things. If there's a mistake or something I don't want in our composition, I just fix it.

I'm very much behind the camera and know exactly what the lens sees, because I set it up. I set the lens and the focal length, so with every single position I know exactly what the frame is. I've just developed that sense. Standing and watching behind the camera, standing where the magazine is going, gives you a kind of axis, a straight line to the center of the picture. I can see whether the camera tilts down too much or whether it's where it should be.

Selecting a camera operator is very important, and when you find a good one you keep that relationship going. At the end of *Five Easy Pieces*, I found Bobby Byrne. He didn't have a long track record, but I decided in our first meeting that he was going to be okay. He worked out very well, and we ended doing 18 pictures together. We went through some trials together, too, because after *Five Easy Pieces* we made *The Last Movie*!

You worked with Bob Rafelson again on *The King of Marvin Gardens*.

Kovacs: We had plenty of time to shoot both *Five Easy Pieces* and *The King of Marvin Gardens*. They were not big-budget movies, but it seemed we had time for everything. We never really felt pressured. We had 10 or 12 weeks, which was a luxury for an independent film in those days. We made *The King of Marvin Gardens* for less than $1 million, our budget concession from the union, so we didn't have to have a full crew.

The King of Marvin Gardens was always my favorite. It's about a dramatic relationship, and it somehow represents everything I look for in a movie. The relationships are tied to the environment, and the relationship between the brothers is very dramatic. Their dream doesn't come true. How blindly you believe in the dream! It's almost like a classic tragedy, especially after one brother gets killed and the hero goes back where he came from.

The film is very intimate. There aren't that many characters, and we get very close to all of them.

Kovacs: Yes, and on a very deep level. The hero is talking about himself, and these are probably his closest and deepest thoughts about when they were kids and their grandfather was putting the little plastic toy in his Crackerjack box. At the end, when the younger brother goes back home, it's really heartbreaking. Somehow, at two or three in the morning, when very few people are listening to his radio program, he is able to reveal himself on the air with a monologue. After this dramatic story, you wonder whether it was a flashback or whether it really happened. His brother suddenly dies, and the next thing you know it's nighttime. His life goes on, but you know that there isn't much happiness or brightness for him. There is only depression.

Did you shoot that in real hotel rooms?

Kovacs: Oh, yes. It all takes place in a hotel in Atlantic City. We blocked out a long scene in the living area of the hotel room. They're not supposed to be there, and the manager comes in and the Bruce Dern character tries to con him. Bob Rafelson said, 'I want to do this scene in one shot.' It was seven minutes long. I said okay and immediately looked around. We were on the tenth floor! I wasn't able to source-light from outside the window, especially in those days, when we didn't have Condors. But even a Condor wouldn't go up to the tenth floor. I leaned against a doorway and held my head, and I said, 'Where am I going to put the lights?' Bob said, 'I left you one corner, didn't I?'

But it actually worked. Every time I see that scene, I cringe and my knuckles turn white. I just can't believe we did that scene in one take. It's very complicated, dramatic and kind of funny, and on top of that the Ellen Burstyn character is screaming at him from the bathroom. It was pandemonium. It has a lot of tension, and that's how it stands up.

It's such a remarkable film. The Ellen Burstyn character is breaking down right in front of your eyes, and so much is foreshadowed. You had very low light levels and were shooting with pretty slow film.

Kovacs: What's important in cinematography is to have total control of the lighting, even in small, confined areas. I had to adapt to the situation and to what the story dictated. Okay, they lived on the tenth floor. There was a dramatic reason for that, probably not the most important, but they had take elevators up and down, so there were scenes in the elevator. They walk into a dark room with no electricity. It's very Chekhovian.

The dramatic elements were very important, like the gun that kept changing hands. It ended up in Bruce Dern's pocket. You know the dramatic law: if there's a gun in the first act, it will go off in the third act. And it did. So there is real significance to that gun. You feel uncomfortable when you see it being passed between people, especially when we cut close to it. Watching it now, I feel at that moment that somebody's going to get shot. I was really scared that gun was going to go off! Throughout the film, nothing is settled. There is an undercurrent of uneasiness.

I took this film to a master class in Hungary. The school requested two films; the first was *Easy Rider*, which had been restored, thank God. They named another title, but I said, 'How about *The King of Marvin Gardens*?' They had never heard of it! It's never been released in Hungary. I told them it would be a very good selection. When the screening was over, they said, 'That's not like an American film. It's like a European movie.' They thought everything about it — the dramatic structure, the acting style, the visuals — was European.

Where does your style come from?

Kovacs: It's very difficult to define. To me, it's pure instinct. I make selections based on what I feel the dramatics dictate. That's why a dramatic film is more important than anything else, including action films and science fiction. Those things don't motivate me any more, even though I can do them. I'm sure a lot of cinematographers feel the same way.

Something has to grab you in the script, even if it's just one simple thing about a character or a relationship, or a couple of moments. That's when I start feeling the tone, the mood, and start becoming fixed on it. Before I get to the actual shooting, I meet with the director and production designer and take all these little steps in the interest of the film.

Locations are incredibly important because you're selecting the environment in which your characters live. It's not just a room to shoot in or a place to go; it has to have a function, and it has to be an organic part of the drama and the people. I understand why directors get so particular about details. I know, and I can see that the director knows, that every single prop has to have meaning to the character. They live there and create their environment.

For me, these things are all inside you by the time you start shooting the film. That's why you can't really prepare. You prepare daily, of course, by making storyboards, floor plans and lighting plans; but how can you actually see it happening until the actors come and start rehearsing? The director works with them, and suddenly the words have meaning and the characters have relationships. Going into a rehearsal I'm ready, and when it's over I know exactly how it should look. I already see the scene on the screen, shot and played. I just have to go and do it. But is duplicating what you've already imagined good enough, or do you want to push the envelope? This question always arises.

How do you light for dramatics?

Kovacs: When you put up the first light and then the next, they logistically start to connect and create the image you're after. In the process of this logic of light, there are absolutely physical laws. You know what happens when you add another light, and suddenly that light gives you another idea. Lighting is such an intimate process in the life of the cinematographer. You can't talk about it when you're doing it because there is no time to share those feelings, even with your operator or gaffer. All you ask for, all you require, is for them to do it. I simply say, 'Please do what I'm asking you to do.' And blind faith makes them do it.

Of course, it's important to be open to suggestion and ideas. But gradually, little by little, the lighting converges and you finally see with the last touch that it's ready. Unfortunately, cinematographers work under such pressure that we don't have the kind of time and luxury that the painter has. The production of every picture translates down to a time element, five minutes, ten minutes. You do the wide shot and the medium shot, and when you get to the close-up they say, 'Can you do that fast?' The close-up is the most important shot. You know, Rembrandt spent so much time on a single close-up! And they ask us to hurry up. You have to learn; you can't fight back. It always turns out that your mind is faster than the words coming out of your mouth.

The close-up has to come out of the other scenes; that way it has complete meaning. Maybe the director is going to throw everything else away and play with just that scene, especially if the actor is good. Some actors save their best effort for the close-up, and they deliver magical moments. The artistic responsibility gets stronger and stronger as you get closer and closer. You know this is where things are really going to count, and you have to be 'there.' You have to help create those characters with light.

That's why cinematography is such a fabulous form of art. You're pulling these incredible images out of all the hardware, cables, lights, stands and frames. You could go on listing the equipment forever, and somewhere in the middle of all that there really is an art. It depends on how you use the tools.

In the good old days of the small films, I learned simplicity. The simpler you are, the more effective, the more demanding and to-the-point you are. I've learned to use as little equipment as I can. Luckily, my gaffer, Aggie, and I grew up in that school where you have to make magic with practically nothing. It took us almost a lifetime to learn that simplicity is always the most effective. A backlight can be a huge bank of 10Ks or HMIs, but it can also be just one light.

Richard Aguilar has been your gaffer on more than 50 films. Tell me about him.

Kovacs: The way Aggie and I communicate is very interesting; it's body language and nonverbal. While we were working on *Mask*, we were in and out of that tiny little house where everything happened. The AD called lunch, and Peter [Bogdanovich] said, 'Let me work on the setup after lunch.' As soon as he said that, Aggie and the best boy stayed. Peter and I started working on the blocking; somebody was coming out of the house, and the camera moved and we did a two-shot. Aggie was standing next to the truck and the best boy was up in the back of the truck, and I swear to God, Aggie started calling the lights. Then Peter said we were going to do a two-shot, and Aggie said, 'HMI.' We worked it out in about 15 minutes, so we still had lunch time. I said to Peter, 'Okay, we'll call you after lunch.' I turned around, and Aggie had everything right there off the truck. I said, 'Exactly right. Let's go have lunch.'

Normally, after you work on a setup with a director you turn to the gaffer and tell him what you need. But Aggie already knew; it was already lined up. Basically, that is very typical of how we work.

How does viewing dailies affect your camerawork?

Kovacs: After we see the first day of dailies, we make little adjustments — you can always improve. It gives us a visual starting place for the next day; it sets up the tones and the moods, and the crew gets the picture. I can't express on set why I'm doing this and that, but when we all watch the dailies we suddenly 'see' it in a giant sense. We can relate to it now.

What happens when you start a different scene, or another location, or maybe a sub-plot with different characters? How do you indicate that it's still the same film? Again, you have that instinct, and now you've seen part of the movie on film, the rest of it is here, in your mind.

You also have, as they say, your individual style. Young filmmakers tell me that they can always tell a Kovacs picture.

Do they tell you what they see that tells them that?

Kovacs: Not really. They can't, because I've never really thought of making two pictures the same. There's no such thing.

That seems to be your philosophy.

Kovacs: Each story carries its own look or light. These kids can just tell. They can tell a Gordon Willis movie or a Caleb Deschanel movie, too. I've been watching Caleb's work like a hawk. Lately, they've been running *The Natural* on cable TV, and I watch it when I wake up. Even on TV, his visual ideas and the lighting look good. His work is unique and noticeable but not contrived. He's smart, you know. He works with light like a juggler, like a magician. It tells the story amazingly. And I know how hard it is to do what he does. They say he's slow. What do you expect, flashlights?! I know why he's slow: he's an artist! It's a miracle that he can put it through with all of those watchdogs. When you're making a film, you can't take shortcuts and expect any kind of reward.

What do you think of film critics?

Kovacs: I am always interested in what reviewers say, but most of the time I wish I'd never read the reviews. They don't know how to judge cinematography, whether it's the greatest film critic or not. They don't know what to say about cinematography, and at best they never say anything about it that I like. They might say the technical side is okay, or the camera is in the right place.

There were a few critics who were interested in the evolution of the Hollywood filmmakers who emerged in the 1960s. It was phenomenal. These low-budget films were made by Bogdanovich, Rafelson, Francis Ford Coppola, Marty Scorsese, Dennis Hopper and William Friedkin, and those names suddenly emerged as the greatest filmmakers in the 1970s, which I consider the greatest decade in American film. Hollywood was such an exciting environment to be in. There were so many things happening. But now, look outside. This town is dead. Creative energy is at its lowest point. In the 1960s this town was alive. All this stuff was happening, especially when the '70s came in and all our New York colleagues, like Owen Roizman and Victor Kemper, came out here. Suddenly we realized we were friends.

We felt we should have more freedom in filmmaking. We all gravitated toward each other and became friendly. It was interesting, because in those days we all had the same agent, who was also a script supervisor. We used to congregate at his house on the beach at

Malibu. Sometimes there were 18 or 20 cinematographers in the same room! We started planning how we should do our own business. There was a great need for change. They elected me president of our group.

Jay Cipes was one of the high-ranking officials at Technicolor back then, and he initiated a Friday evening screening series for cinematographers at the lab. With the studios' permission, films that were two or three weeks away from release were shown to our group. We met for dinner and started the screenings at 7 o'clock. The screening room wasn't big, maybe 25 seats, but it was full of friends, wives and everybody. And I tell you, the cinematographer was under a magnifier after it was over! You were either going through a grinder or getting compliments.

We were able to criticize each other and talk about each other's work. We would say, 'That scene was so incredible. How did you do it?' It was just unbelievable. We were all working with one of these new young directors. Some of us were so close that if we had a script we didn't really like, we were able to trade projects. There were several times when we were able to switch by talking the director into using somebody else. Vilmos would say, 'Why don't you try Laszlo?'

Our group was so active in those days. I still have those wonderful relationships; they have been transposed completely to the ASC. The contemporary ASC is basically the generation that started working in the 1960s. And of course, we have a new generation coming in. Our function has changed a little bit in that we focus more on education. The next generation will have young cinematographers just starting out, and we'll be holding master classes, workshops, seminars, whatever we can.

I've got a speech ready for the new ASC Clubhouse. I can hardly wait for the ASC to have a screening room. Then we can do something we can't do today. We can invite film-school classes to come hear not one cinematographer, but six or eight. We can set up screenings and invite different cinematographers. This kind of outreach is extremely important for the future.

I've heard that you met Orson Welles while you were working on *Paper Moon*, and he told you to shoot black-and-white film with a red filter.

Kovacs: Yes. It was a short meeting but memorable. He told me to see his film *Chimes at Midnight*. He said he had used arc lights at night for all those battle scenes and the castle, and he had used a red filter on the lens. He said the cinematographer begged him not to use it, but he said the production had all of the arc lights that there were in Europe. That's what he had to do at night to duplicate the daylight and the blue balance. That's when the red filter really works. Taking the red out makes skin tones very chalky, and the blues, of course, go dark.

So you used arc lights with daylight exteriors on *Paper Moon*?

Kovacs: Yes. Peter was uncompromising about depth of field. The image had to be sharp from the closest object to the farthest object in the frame. It was a big challenge. It's not just a lot of light, but you also have to feel that it's a low-light-level, dramatic situation. Light couldn't just pour in; it had to be modeled and look real.

We were always shooting at T8 and trying to get to a T11. There's a very close-up shot in the night scene where Tatum O'Neal is in the carnival, buying cotton candy and walking down to the Ferris wheel. Peter said, 'I want that Ferris wheel in the shot.' My assistant kept telling me he couldn't carry focus. I was up to T11. Aggie was borrowing generators from all the rides. We finally said, 'That's it.' I told my assistant to put it on T16 and push it one stop.

In those days, there were no HMIs for night-time or a tungsten situation with interiors. Even if there had been, I would have been very hesitant to use them, because small tungsten units are easier to control in interiors. I tested the black-and-white film with an orange filter, because it occurred to me that panchromatic film is sensitive to tungsten light. It basically enhances the tungsten and converts the daylight to a certain degree of tungsten sensitivity. So I figured that a #1 orange has a lot of red and a lot of warmth, and it probably does the same thing with an exterior that the blue light does when you're using a red filter. And I tell you, it was a perfect match. That way I only lost one stop, and that's much better than losing three stops!

How did you come to work with Scorsese on *New York, New York*?

Kovacs: That was a major studio musical and a big production. I had a phone call from Marty, asking me to meet him at a little bistro on Sunset Boulevard. He was just finishing another film, and he said he just wanted to talk to me a little bit. By that time he was already a name to contend with; it was after *Taxi Driver* and *Alice Doesn't Live Here Anymore.* I really love *Alice.* It's a road picture, which for some reason I can always relate to. So I met him at the restaurant and we began talking about the great Hollywood musicals. He said, 'I'm planning a tribute to these musicals, but I'm doing a contemporary drama with it,' and he asked me to do the movie. I was excited to be working with him and doing a musical, something I'd always loved.

This was after I had shot *At Long Last Love,* a musical with Cybill Shepherd and Burt Reynolds, for Peter Bogdanovich. That was a very important experience for me. Peter and I tried to make it interesting visually, and it was a big disappointment for us that it didn't succeed. Peter had the idea of using live recordings of the voices and blending the dialogue with the song.

New York, New York was done in the traditional way, with prerecorded singing. I'll never forget the moment when we were supposed to film Liza Minnelli's performance of the title song. All these extras were ordered to fill in the Rainbow Room, where they were sitting around tables. They hadn't even finished recording the song! They'd been working on it all night, and they finished at four in the morning. They rushed to the studio, where we had been waiting since 7 o'clock the night before, and set up the speakers for the playback all over the stages. Liza and all the musicians arrived and poured out of a van. They were exhausted, and they all looked tired. The conductor had the tape in his hand, and he gave it to the sound man. Everybody stood there as it started playing. It was so terrific, such an exciting song, that when it was over there was a big silence, and then everybody went just crazy. There was such thunderous applause! I still get goosebumps thinking about. I think they played the song six or seven times.

In the meantime, Marty pulled me aside and said, 'This really needs a great entrance.' So we looked around and figured out where Bobby De Niro would be sitting and where Liza would be on the stage. Marty came up with the idea of having De Niro weave through the tables as we see Liza way in the background. At that time there was no Steadicam, so we set up a long track for a big crane; we could follow De Niro with the crane arm and swing forward. We could take it right to his table, and by then we'd be a little bit behind him and Liza would be visible up on the stage.

We had a problem in that Liza didn't have her final wardrobe. Thea Van Runkel was the wardrobe designer, and she had some different ideas. I said Liza needed to be in something very light and feminine, because when we start with the shot way back in the room we have to see her up on the stage. Thea brought out this soft, red fabric that you could almost see through, and she could kind of wrap it around Liza's upper body. She said, 'How about this with black pants?' I said it was great.

That scene was also an enormous lighting job. I told Aggie that the only way to make the huge space interesting was to backlight every shot, even the reverses. There were 50 or 60 10Ks on Stage 30 at MGM, one of the largest stages. So it took us a long time.

There was so much to that movie. Marty speaks, but his mind is about a mile ahead, and he's always trying to catch up with his own thinking. He's always so far ahead of what he's talking about. He was very well prepared on that film, but he never really trusted his preparedness.

***Frances* is a heartbreaking story. What was your approach to lighting that film?**

Kovacs: Yes, it's very tough. At the same time, it's one of the most satisfying films I've done because I love the character of Frances Farmer and her relationship with her mother. One way I had to use light was to indicate how Frances aged over the course of the story. Filming her as a high-school girl was the hardest and shortest section to do.

In each section of the film, something devastating happens to her. Her life was like a Beethoven sonata — she would go somewhere, like off to Hollywood or New York, but she'd always end up back at home. Her tragedy was that she wasn't able to break away. We lit the Farmer home to be very warm, even when her mother was there. It always has that warm, cozy feeling, and when Frances goes out into the world, those places look cold. Every time she goes home, she sees the warmth. This is how we tell stories without words.

Nowadays you're shooting romantic comedies like *Return to Me* and *Miss*

Congeniality. **How do you feel about making comedies?**

Kovacs: I feel very good about it. You know, it's not easy to shoot a comedy, and it's not easy for actors to do comedy. The director has to be very good. A romantic comedy basically has to be about people who are as real as possible. We're trying to create as much reality around the characters as possible.

It was the same with *Ghostbusters.* I never really believed anyone was going to laugh at that movie, and I was so wrong! You know, kids are really good critics. I have a daughter who's a film buff, and she loves *Ghostbusters.* She first saw it on VHS, and she was roaring. She still loves it.

When I do a comedy, I always think about what the human elements are. Of course, the goals of a comedy are very different than those of a drama. But I still have to create the world around the characters. If the ambiance isn't real, the audience isn't going to buy the actors.

I remember a time when I was working with an actor who was just too overbearing, with too much physical presence. I asked someone to give me a baseball cap, and I said to the actor, 'I think this would be really great for your character. Look at the shape of the cap. I can light you in way that you can control with it. Widen your eyes to convey strength to the other character. If you tilt your head down, your eyes will get dark and menacing. If you take the cap off, you'll just have a bare head.' Well, he loved it. And it worked.

Multiplicity was a very different kind of comedy. Digital techniques were used organically to tell a story about a man and his three clones. Hats off to Michael Keaton, who understood the digital process. The picture was so demanding; he had to go in and out of character at the snap of a finger. He was extremely inventive. He played totally different characters, and it was a great challenge to make him look like four different actors. And they all had to walk around each other! The complications of using motion-control and greenscreen were amazing, and it took a long time to work out the details.

The director, Harold Ramis, and I knew going in that we had to storyboard the film very carefully. We spent six weeks at a big table with all the visual-effects people, and we went through the visual-effects sequences scene by scene. Harold had to decide the blocking right then, and each shot, each setup, had to be timed. The studio wouldn't let us start shooting until we had determined a visual-effects budget. Harold is a very conscientious director. He was conscious of our budget, the physical logistics and the physical problems. Of course, we got bolder and bolder later on, while we were shooting the movie. Instead of doing five setups, sometimes we did it all in one!

Your film *Radio Flyer* seems to have completely disappeared from the public's mind. Why is that?

Kovacs: I don't know. It's one of my favorite films. I think it's wonderful. Richard Donner did a beautiful job creating a story about child abuse.

It's a tough subject to sell.

Kovacs: Yes, and on top of that I think the marketing department screwed up. The advertisements made you think it was a children's movie. Remember the poster? It had two beautiful kids with a red wagon and a German shepherd. It looked like a Disney movie. Totally misleading.

How do you tell the story of a film?

Kovacs: I always try to find the visual language for the story I'm trying to photograph. That's what the cinematographer's tool is. I tell the story of the characters visually. Throughout my career I've favored people-oriented movies as opposed to action and science fiction. Of course, I've dabbled in those genres, too. I did a few action movies just to see what it was like, and they never really satisfied me. I just keep returning to people-motivated stories, whether it's drama or romantic comedy.

At this point I've been locked into another pigeonhole as a romantic comedy specialist, thanks to *My Best Friend's Wedding, Return to Me* and *Miss Congeniality.* But I really don't mind. I feel good about portraying a man and a woman in love.

A cinematographer can do any kind of film, and in the course of a career it's good to do things that are different. You can't always be in a position to do exactly what you like. That's too much to ask. I'm grateful to be a cinematographer.

Kovacs filming handheld on San Francisco's Haight Street with director Richard Rush for *Psych-Out* (1968).

Laszlo Kovacs Filmography

(Director of Photography)

1. *Incredibly Strange Creatures Who Stopped Living and Became Mixed-Up Zombies, The* (1963)
... aka Diabolical Dr. Voodoo (1963)
... aka Incredibly Mixed Up Zombie, The (1963)
... aka Incredibly Strange Creature: Or Why I Stopped Living and Became a Mixed-up Zombie, The (1963) (USA)
... aka Teenage Psycho Meets Bloody Mary, The (1963)

Zero-budget cult classic about a bizarre carnival with monsters and rock 'n' roll. Atmospheric but thin story features brilliant colors, abysmal acting, ridiculous dialogue and great cinematography. Definitely of the "so bad it's great" variety, with one of the finest titles ever to grace a motion picture.

Directed by Ray Dennis Steckler
Writing credits – E.M. Kevke (story), Gene Pollock, Robert Silliphant

Cast
Carolyn Brandt – Marge Neilson
Toni Camel – Stella
Erina Enyo – Carmelita
Ray Dennis Steckler – Jerry (as Cash Flagg)
Atlas King – Harold
Brett O'Hara – Madame Estrella
Gene Pollock – Night Club Manager
Produced by Ray Dennis Steckler
Original music by Henri Price, Libby Quinn
Cinematography by Laszlo Kovacs, Joseph V. Mascelli, Vilmos Zsigmond
Film Editing by Don Schneider

2. *Kiss Me Quick!* (1964)
... aka Dr. Breedlove (1964)
... aka Dr. Breedlove or: How I Learned to Stop Worrying and Love (1964)

Monsters and semi-clad go-go dancers mix it up in this Nudie Cutie horror comedy that features appearances by Dracula, Frankenstein and the Mummy. A dimwitted alien named Sterilox searches for "the perfect female specimen" in the castle of Dr. Breedlove.

Directed by Max Gardens
Writing credits – Peter Perry

Cast
Claudia Banks – Hotty Totty
Fred Coe – Sterilox
Althea Currier – Gertie Tassle
Jackie De Witt – Kissme
Max Gardens – Dr. Breedlove
Produced by Harry H. Novak
Cinematography by Laszlo Kovacs
Other crew – William Rotsler – still photographer

3. *National Geographic Specials* (1964)
TV Series

Directed by Alexander Grasshoff

Cast
Alexander Scourby – Narrator
Produced by Nick Cominos
Original music by Arthur Morton
Cinematography by Laszlo Kovacs
Film Editing by Bud Friedgen

4. *Time-Life Specials: The March of Time* (1965) TV Series

Directed by William T. Cartwright
Writing credits – James L.Brooks

Cast
William Conrad – Narrator (voice)
Produced by William T. Cartwright
Original music by Elmer Bernstein
Cinematography by Laszlo Kovacs
Film Editing by David E. Blewitt

5. *Smell of Honey, a Swallow of Brine, A* (1966)

Exploitation master David F. Friedman's "roughie" tale of young girl's search for happiness in and out of clothing with a variety of unappreciative clods.

Directed by Byron Mabe (as B. Ron Elliot)
Writing credits – David F. Friedman

Cast
Stacey Walker – Sharon Winters
Neville Coward – Lowell Carter
Bob Todd – Tony
Sharon Carr – Paula
Michael Wright – Mr. Gordon
Michael O'Kelly – Roy
Larry N. Jones
Produced by David F. Friedman
Original music by Et Cetera, Mark Wayne
Cinematography by Laszlo Kovacs (as Art Radford)
Film Editing by Byron Mabe

6. *Notorious Daughter of Fanny Hill, The* (1966)

Very limited budget for this exploitation version of a sequel to erotic classic. Veteran shlockmeisters Friedman and Sonney teamed up for this one.

Directed by Peter Perry

Cast
John Andrews
Linda Cochran (as Leigh Cochran)
Tom Duncan
Letitia Farrell
Stacey Walker – Kissy Hill
Produced by David F. Friedman and Dan Sonney
Cinematography by Laszlo Kovacs
Other crew William Rotsler – still photographer

7. *Man Called Dagger, A* (1967)

Low-budget attempt to crash the spy-movie cycle that was big in the 1960s. This was the first of several collaborations between Kovacs and director Richard Rush. Look for Richard "Jaws" Kiel in one of his earliest roles.

Directed by Richard Rush
Writing credits – James Peatman, Robert S. Weekley

Cast
Paul Mantee – Dick Dagger
Terry Moore – Harper Davis
Jan Murray – Rudolph
Koffman/Hans Leitel – Sue Ane Langdon
Ingrid Eileen O'Neill – Erica
Maureen Arthur – Joy
Leonard Stone – Karl Rainer
Richard Kiel – Otto
Produced by Lew Horwitz, Richard Rush
Original music by Steve Allen
Cinematography by Laszlo Kovacs
Film Editing by Tom Boutross

8. *Hell's Angels on Wheels* (1967)

Jack Nicholson as a gas-station attendant who joins up with the motorcycle gang. One of the better biker films of the 1960s. Director Rush explores a Faustian theme in a contemporary context.

Directed by Richard Rush
Writing credits – R. Wright Campbell

Cast
Adam Roarke – Buddy
Jack Nicholson – Poet
Sabrina Scharf – Shill
Jana Taylor – Abigale
Richard Anders – Bull
John Garwood – Jock
I.J. Jefferson – Pearl
James Oliver – Gypsy

Sonny Barger – Himself
Produced by Joe Solomon
Original music by Stu Phillips
Cinematography by Laszlo Kovacs (as Leslie Kovacs)
Film Editing by William Martin

9. *Blood of Dracula's Castle* (1967)

... aka Castle of Dracula (1967)
... aka Dracula's Castle (1967) (USA: TV title)

Awesomely bad horror movie about a couple who inherit a castle and find that Mr. and Mrs. Dracula still reside there – and keep a fresh supply of virgins chained up in the dungeon.

Directed by Al Adamson
Writing credits – Rex Carlton

Cast
Alexander D'Arcy – Count Dracula, alias Count Charles Townsend
Paula Raymond – Countess Townsend
Gene O'Shane – Glen Cannon
Barbara Bishop – Liz Arden
Robert Dix – Johnny
John Carradine – George, the Butler
Produced by Al Adamson
Original music by Lincoln Mayorage
Cinematography by Laszlo Kovacs (as Leslie Kovacs)
Film Editing by Peter Perry Jr.

10. *Psych-Out* (1968)

A real 1960s time piece. A girl joins up with the hippies in San Francisco. Actually shot on location on Haight Street. Great psychedelic visual effects and classic soundtrack (originally available as LP), with music by Mike Bloomfield.

Directed by Richard Rush
Writing credits – Betty Tusher (also story) Betty Ulius, E. Hunter Willett

Cast
Susan Strasberg – Jenny
Dean Stockwell – Dave
Jack Nicholson – Stoney
Bruce Dern – Steve
Adam Roarke – Ben
Max Julien – Elwood
Henry Jaglom – Warren
Linda Gaye Scott – Lynn
I.J. Jefferson – Pandora
Tommy Flanders – Wesley
Ken Scott – Preacher
Produced by Dick Clark
Original music by Ronald Stein and Mike Bloomfield
Cinematography by Laszlo Kovacs
Film Editing by Renn Reynolds

11. *Targets* (1968)

... aka Before I Die (1968)

Prescient tale of a sniper at a drive-in. Great example of fine storytelling and cinematography on a limited budget. One of Karloff's last motion pictures; he plays a horror-film star making a personal appearance at a drive-in movie premiere.

Directed by Peter Bogdanovich
Writing credits – Polly Platt and Peter Bogdanovich, Samuel Fuller (uncredited) (story) Orson Welles (uncredited)

Cast
Tim O'Kelly – Bobby Thompson
Boris Karloff – Byron Orlok
Arthur Peterson – Ed Loughlin
Monte Landis – Marshall Smith
Nancy Hsueh – Jenny
Peter Bogdanovich – Sammy Michaels
Produced by Peter Bogdanovich
Original music by Charles Greene, Brian Stone
Cinematography by Laszlo Kovacs
Film Editing by Peter Bogdanovich

12. *Single Room Furnished* (1968)

Jayne Mansfield goes from innocence and pregnancies to prostitution in this film, adapted from a Gerald Sanford play. The actress died in a car accident before the film was completed.

Directed by Matt Cimber
Writing credits – Michael Musto,

Gerald Sanford (play)

Cast
Jayne Mansfield – Eileen
Dorothy Keller
Fabian Dean
Billy M. Greene
Terry Messina
Martin Horsey
Walter Gregg
Bruno VeSota
Velia Del Greco – Mrs. Adamo
Isabelle Dwan – Grandmother
Produced by Hugo Grimaldi
Original music by James Sheldon
Cinematography by Laszlo Kovacs
Film Editing by Hugo Grimaldi

13. *Savage Seven, The* (1968)

Cult film about a motorcycle gang riding into Indian town controlled by corrupt businessmen. Bikers attempt to help the Indians. Zoom street cinematography and Reynolds' "flash forward" editing presage *Easy Rider*.

Directed by Richard Rush
Writing credits – Michael Fisher, Rosalind Ross (story)

Cast
Robert Walker Jr. – Johnnie
Joanna Frank – Marcia
John Garwood – Stud
Larry Bishop – Joint
Adam Roarke – Kisum
Max Julien – Grey Wolf
Richard Anders – Bull
Duane Eddy – Eddie
Charles Bail – Taggert (as Chuck Bail)
Penny Marshall – Tina
Produced by Samuel Z. Arkoff, Dick Clark, James H. Nicholson
Original music by Mike Curb
Cinematography by Laszlo Kovacs
Film Editing by Renn Reynolds

14. *Mantis in Lace* (1968)
... aka Lila (1968)

Go-go dancer turns serial killer while tripping on LSD. Real hip dialogue.

Directed by William Rotsler
Writing credits – Sanford White

Cast
Susan Stewart – Lila
Steve Vincent – Sergeant Collins
M.K. Evans – Lieutenant Ryan
Vic Lance – Tiger
Pat Barrington – Cathy
Janu Wine – Angel
Stuart Lancaster – Frank
John Caroll – Ben
John LaSalle – Fred
Hinton Pope – Chief Barnes
Bethel G. Buckalew – Bartender
Lyn Armondo – Real Estate Woman
Norton Halper – Tenant
Judith Crane – Dancer
Cheryl Trepton – Dancer
Produced by Harry H. Novak, Peter Perry, Sanford White
Original music by Frank A. Coe, Lynn Harper (song)
Cinematography by Laszlo Kovacs (as Leslie Kovacks)
Film Editing by Peter Perry Jr.

15. *Easy Rider* (1969)

Landmark film about two hippies searching for America on a motorcycle trip across the country. Generally viewed as the film that ushered in the American New Wave of the 1970s.

Directed by Dennis Hopper
Writing credits – Peter Fonda, Dennis Hopper and Terry Southern

Cast
Peter Fonda – Wyatt (Captain America)
Dennis Hopper – Billy
Antonio Mendoza – Jesus
Phil Spector – Connection

Mac Mashourian – Bodyguard
Warren Finnerty – Rancher
Tita Colorado – Rancher's Wife
Luke Askew – Stranger on Highway
Luana Anders – Lisa
Sabrina Scharf – Sarah
Robert Walker Jr. – Jack (as Robert Walker)
Jack Nicholson – George Hanson
Produced by Peter Fonda
Original music by Hoyt Axton (song "The Pusher"), Mars Bonfire (song "Born To Be Wild")
Cinematography by Laszlo Kovacs
Film Editing by Donn Cambern

16. *That Cold Day in the Park* (1969)

Unhappy, obssessive woman gives shelter to young man from nearby park.

Directed by Robert Altman
Writing credits – Gillian Freeman

Cast
Sandy Dennis – Frances Austen
Michael Burns – The boy
Susanne Benton – Nina
David Garfield – Nick (as John Garfield Jr.)
Luana Anders – Sylvie
Michael Murphy – The Rounder
Edward Greenhalgh – The doctor
Linda Sorenson – The prostitute
Produced by Robert Eggenweiler, Donald Factor, Leon Mirell
Original music by Johnny Mandel
Cinematography by Laszlo Kovacs
Film Editing by Danford B. Greene

17. *Making of the President 1968* (1969) (TV)

Directed by Mel Stuart
Writing credits – Theodore White

Cast
Joseph Campanella – Narrator
Produced by Mel Stuart
Cinematography by Laszlo Kovacs
Film Editing by David Saxon

18. *Day with the Boys, A* (1969)

Directed by Clu Gulager
Writing credits – Clu Gulager

Cast
Ricky Bender
Artie Conkling
William Elliott
Jack Grindle
John Gulager
Mike Hertel
James Kearce
John McCaffrey
Mark Spirtos
Greg Williams
Produced by Clu Gulager
Cinematography by Laszlo Kovacs

19. *Hell's Bloody Devils* (1970)

... aka Fakers, The (1970) (USA: TV title)
... aka Operation M. (1970)
... aka Smashing the Crime Syndicate (1970) (UK)
... aka Swastika Savages (1970)

Neo-Nazis, sadistic bikers and the mob mix it up with the evil Count von Delberg. Very close to so-bad-it's-good, with lots of violence.

Directed by Al Adamson
Writing credits – Jerry Evans

Cast
John Gabriel – Mark Adams
Anne Randall – Amanda
Broderick Crawford – Brand
Scott Brady – F.B.I. Agent
Kent Taylor – Count von Delberg
Robert Dix – Cunk
Keith Andes – Bremonte
John Carradine – Merchant
Produced by Al Adamson
Original music by Don McGinnis, Nelson Riddle
Cinematography by Gary Graver, Laszlo Kovacs
Film Editing by John Winfield

20. *Getting Straight* (1970)

Campus riots of the 1960s with Elliott Gould as returning war vet in the middle of it all. More '60s time-capsule filmmaking from Richard Rush.

Directed by Richard Rush
Writing credits – Robert Kaufman, Ken Kolb (novel)

Cast
Elliott Gould – Harry Bailey
Candice Bergen – Jan
Robert F. Lyons – Nick
Jeff Corey – Dr. Willhunt
Max Julien – Ellis
Cecil Kellaway – Dr. Kasper
Produced by Paul Lewis
Original music by Ronald Stein
Cinematography by Laszlo Kovacs
Film Editing by Maury Winetrobe

21. *Five Easy Pieces* (1970)

Jack Nicholson as musician who has given up the piano to work on oil fields. A superb film, and the intimate story was a breakthrough for Kovacs.

Directed by Bob Rafelson
Writing credits – Carole Eastman, (also story) (as Adrien Joyce) Bob Rafelson (story)

Cast
Jack Nicholson –Bobby Dupea
Karen Black – Rayette Dipesto
Billy Green Bush – Elton (as Billy 'Green' Bush)
Fannie Flagg – Stoney
Sally Struthers – Betty (as Sally Ann Struthers)
Marlena MacGuire – Twinky
Richard Stahl – Recording Engineer
Lois Smith – Partita Dupea
Helena Kallianiotes – Palm Apodaca
Toni Basil – Terry Grouse
Lorna Thayer – Waitress
Susan Anspach – Catherine Van Oost
Ralph Waite – Carl Fidelio Dupea
William Challee – Nicholas Dupea
John P. Ryan – Spicer (as John Ryan)
Irene Dailey – Samia Glavia
Produced by Bob Rafelson, Bert Schneider
Music by Johann Sebastian Bach, Frédéric Chopin, Wolfgang Amadeus Mozart
Cinematography by Laszlo Kovacs
Film Editing by Christopher Holmes

22. *Rebel Rousers, The* (1970)

Motorcycle gang takes over town where drag race is being held. Jack Nicholson, in striped pants, stands out.

Directed by Martin B. Cohen
Writing credits – Martin B. Cohen, Michael Kars, Abe Polsky

Cast
Cameron Mitchell – Paul Collier
Bruce Dern – J.J. Weston
Diane Ladd – Karen
Jack Nicholson – Bunny
Harry Dean Stanton – Randolph Halverson
Neil Burstyn – Rebel
Lou Procopio – Rebel
Earl Finn – Rebel
Philip Carey – Rebel
Robert Dix – Miguel
Produced by Dascha Auberbach
Original music by William Loose
Cinematography by Laszlo Kovacs
Glen R. Smith
Film Editing by George W. Brooks

23. *Alex in Wonderland* (1970)

Semi-autobiographical satire about a young director (based on Mazursky, played by Donald Sutherland) who is trying to make a film that nobody will watch. Look for cameos by Fellini and Jeanne Moreau.

Directed by Paul Mazursky
Writing credits – Paul Mazursky & Larry Tucker

Cast
Donald Sutherland – Alex
Ellen Burstyn – Beth
Meg Mazursky – Amy
Glenna Sargent – Nancy

Viola Spolin – Mother
Andre Philippe – Andre
Michael Lerner – Leo
Joan Delaney – Jane
Paul Mazursky – Hal Stern
Angelo Rossitto – Fellini #1
John Rico – Fellini #2
Howlett Smith – Piano Player
Virginia Hawkins – Secretary
Dick Geary – Studio Cop (as Richard Geary)
Frances E. Nealy – Maid (as Frances Nealy)
Billy Holms – P.R. Man
George Reynolds – Chauffeur
Federico Fellini – Himself
Jeanne Moreau – Herself
Produced by Anthony Ray
Original music by Tom O'Horgan
Cinematography by Laszlo Kovacs
Film Editing by Stuart H. Pappé

24. *Marriage of a Young Stockbroker, The* (1971)

Tragi-comic story of marriage on the rocks with voyeur husband and troubled wife. Adapted from novel by Charles Webb, who also wrote *The Graduate.*

Directed by Lawrence Turman
Writing credits – Lorenzo Semple Jr., Charles Webb (novel)

Cast
Richard Benjamin – William Alren
Joanna Shimkus – Lisa Alren
Elizabeth Ashley – Nan
Adam West – Chester
Patricia Barry – Doctor Sadler
Tiffany Bolling – Girl in the Rain
Ed Prentiss – Mr. Franklin
Produced by Lawrence Turman
Original music by Fred Karlin
Cinematography by Laszlo Kovacs
Film Editing by Fredric Steinkamp

25. *Last Movie, The* (1971)

... aka Chinchero (1971)

Movie stuntman remains in Peru after film job. Reflexive film about filmmaking that features tons of cameos.

Directed by Dennis Hopper
Writing credits – Dennis Hopper (story), Stewart Stern

Cast
Dennis Hopper – Kansas
Stella Garcia – Maria
Julie Adams – Mrs.Anderson
Tomas Milian – Priest
Don Gordon – Neville Robey
Roy Engel – Harry Anderson
Donna Baccala – Miss Anderson
Samuel Fuller – Himself
Poupée Bocar – Night—club Singer
Sylvia Miles – Script Clerk
Daniel Ades – Thomas Mercado
John Alderman – Jonathan
Michael Anderson Jr. – Mayor's Son
Richmond L. Aguilar – Gaffer
Produced by Michael Gruskoff
Original music by Severn Darden, Chabuca Granda, Kris Kristofferson, John Buck Wilkin
Cinematography by Laszlo Kovacs
Film Editing by David Berlatsky

26. *Pocket Money* (1972)

Modern comic Western about hardluck cowboys trying to get work with crooked rancher. Entertaining vehicle for some great actors.

Directed by Stuart Rosenberg
Writing credits – J.P.S. Brown (novel Jim Kane), John Gay, Terrence Malick

Cast
Paul Newman – Jim Kane
Lee Marvin – Leonard
Strother Martin – Garrett
Christine Belford – Adelita
Kelly Jean Peters – The Wife
Fred Graham – Herb
Wayne Rogers – Stretch Russell
Hector Elizondo – Juan
R. Camargo – Don Tomas

Wynn Pearce – Border Patrolman
Gregory Sierra – Chavarin (as Gregg Sierra)
John Verros – Almara
Bruce Davis Bayne – Bank customer (uncredited)
Richard Farnsworth
Terrence Malick – Worksman (uncredited)
Produced by John Foreman
Original music by Carole King, (title song), Alex North
Cinematography by Laszlo Kovacs
Film Editing by Bob Wyman

27. *What's Up, Doc?* (1972)

Sterling screwball comedy sparked by confusion over identical travel bags. Ryan O'Neal as shy musicologist, Madeline Kahn (in her screen debut) as his strident fiancée and Barbra Streisand as the carefree spirit who comes between them. Also noteworthy for being Kovacs' last Technicolor dye-transfer film; the process was discontinued in the early 1970s.

Directed by Peter Bogdanovich
Writing credits – Peter Bogdanovich (story), Buck Henry, David Newman and Robert Benton

Cast
Barbra Streisand – Judy Maxwell
Ryan O'Neal – Howard Bannister
Madeline Kahn – Eunice Burns
Kenneth Mars – Hugh Simon
Austin Pendleton – Frederick Larrabee
Michael Murphy – Mr. Smith
Philip Roth – Mr. Jones
Sorrell Booke – Harry
Stefan Gierasch – Fritz
Mabel Albertson – Mrs. Van Hoskins
Liam Dunn – Judge Maxwell
John Hillerman – Mr. Kaltenborn
Sean Morgan – Official
Patricia O'Neal – Lady on Plane
Produced by Peter Bogdanovich
Original music by Artie Butler
Cinematography by Laszlo Kovacs
Film Editing by Verna Fields

28. *Slither* (1972)

Frantic chase scenes as James Caan and Peter Boyle scheme to recover big money stolen years prior.

Directed by Howard Zieff
Writing credits – W.D. Richter

Cast
James Caan – Dick Kanipsia
Peter Boyle – Barry Fenaka
Sally Kellerman – Kitty Kopetzky
Louise Lasser – Mary Fenaka
Allen Garfield – Vincent J. Palmer
Richard B. Shull – Harry Moss
Alex Rocco – Man with Ice Cream
Seamon Glass – Farmer in Truck
Produced by W.D. Richter
Original music by Tom McIntosh
Cinematography by Laszlo Kovacs
Film Editing by David Bretherton

29. *King of Marvin Gardens, The* (1972)

A masterful drama about broken dreams and family relations. Jack Nicholson is radio talk jock and Bruce Dern is his schemer brother working for crime syndicate. Kovacs' *Le Bout de Souffle*, intimate filmmaking with high emotional impact.

Directed by Bob Rafelson
Writing credits – Jacob Brackman and Bob Rafelson

Cast
Jack Nicholson – David Staebler
Bruce Dern – Jason Staebler
Ellen Burstyn – Sally
Julia Anne Robinson – Jessica
Scatman Crothers Lewis (as Benjamin 'Scatman' Crothers)
Charles LaVine – Grandfather
Arnold Williams – Rosko
Produced by Bob Rafelson
Cinematography by Laszlo Kovacs
Film Editing by John F. Link

30. *Steelyard Blues* (1973)

... aka Final Crash, The (1973) (USA: TV title)

Crew of misfits tries to steal WWII airplane. Lots of talent, lots of gags.

Directed by Alan Myerson
Writing credits – David S. Ward

Cast
Mel Stewart – Black Man in Jail
Donald Sutherland – Jesse Veldini
Howard Hesseman – Frank Veldini/Frank Veldin
Morgan Upton – Police Captain Bill
Peter Boyle – Eagle Thornberry
Jessica Myerson – Savage Rose
Dan Barrows – Rocky
John Savage – Kid, Jesse's younger brother
Jane Fonda – Iris Caine, Hooker
Nancy Fish – Pool Hall Waitress
Roger Bowen – Fire Commisioner Francis
Garry Goodrow – Duval Jax, Pilot/Mechanic
Lynette Bernay – Bar Waitress
Produced by Tony Bill
Original music by Paul Butterfield, Nick Gravenites, David Shire
Cinematography by Laszlo Kovacs, Stevan Larner
Film Editing by Donn Cambern, Robert Grovener

31. *Reflection of Fear, A* (1973)

... aka Autumn Child (1973)
... aka Labyrinth (1973)

Psychological chiller about young girl's jealous reaction to her father's new girlfriend.

Directed by William A. Fraker
Writing Credits – John Lewis Carlino, Stanton Forbes (novel: Go To Thy Deathbed), Edward Hume

Cast
Robert Shaw – Michael
Sally Kellerman – Anne
Mary Ure – Katherine
Sondra Locke – Marguerite
Signe Hasso – Julia
Mitch Ryan – Inspector McKenna
Gordon Devol – Hector
Gordon Anderson – Aaron (voice)
Victoria Risk – Peggy Leonard
Produced by Howard B.Jaffe
Original music by Fred Myrow
Cinematography by Laszlo Kovacs
Film Editing by Richard K. Brockway

32. *Paper Moon* (1973)

Depression-era tale with Ryan O'Neal as Bible-thumping con man and Tatum O'Neal as a 9-year-old orphan who is better at the sting than he is. Tatum won Oscar for Best Supporting Actress.

Directed by Peter Bogdanovich
Writing credits – Joe David Brown (novel), Alvin Sargent

Cast
Ryan O'Neal – Moses Pray
Tatum O'Neal – Addie Loggins
Madeline Kahn – Trixie Delight
John Hillerman – Deputy Sheriff
Hardin/Jess Hardin
P.J. Johnson – Imogene
Jessie Lee Fulton – Miss Ollie
James N. Harrell – Minister (as Jim Harrell)
Lila Waters – Minister's Wife
Noble Willingham – Mr. Robertson
Produced by Peter Bogdanovich
Cinematography by Laszlo Kovacs
Film Editing by Verna Fields

33. *For Pete's Sake* (1974)

... aka July Pork Bellies (1974)

Comedy with Barbra Streisand trying to get money together to send her husband to school.

Directed by Peter Yates
Writing credits – Stanley Shapiro and Maurice Richlin

Cast
Barbra Streisand – Henrietta 'Henry' Robbins
Michael Sarrazin – Pete Robbins
Estelle Parsons – Helen Robbins
Molly Picon – Mrs. Cherry
William Redfield – Fred Robbins
Louis Zorich – Nick, the dispatcher
Heywood Hale Broun – Judge Hiller
Richard Ward – Bernie

Ed Bakey – Angelo
Peter Mamakos – Dominic
Vivian Bonnell – Loretta
Joseph Maher – Mr. Coates (as Joe Maher)
Anne Ramsey – Telephone Lady
Jack Hollander – Loanshark
Produced by Martin Erlichman
Original music by Artie Butler, Mark Lindsay (main theme)
Cinematography by Laszlo Kovacs
Film Editing by Frank P. Keller

34. *Freebie and the Bean* (1974)

Great car chases and lowbrow humor as two San Francisco cops trash the city while tracking down a mobster. Look for Valerie Harper as Bean's wife.

Directed by Richard Rush
Writing credits Robert Kaufman

Cast
Alan Arkin – Bean
James Caan – Freebie
Loretta Swit – Meyers' Wife
Jack Kruschen – Red Meyers
Mike Kellin – Lt. Rosen
Paul Koslo – Whitey
Linda Marsh – Freebie's Girl
John Garwood – Chauffeur
Alex Rocco – D.A.
Valerie Harper – Bean's Wife, Consuela
Christopher Morley – Transvestite
Bruce Mackey – Floorwalker
Produced by Floyd Mutrux
Original music by Dominic Frontiere
Cinematography by Laszlo Kovacs

35. *Huckleberry Finn* (1974)

... aka Mark Twain's Huckleberry Finn: A Musical Adaptation (1974) (USA: promotional title)

Musical version of classic Mark Twain tale about young boy and runaway slave traversing the Mississippi River.

Directed by J. Lee Thompson
Writing credits – Mark Twain (novel: The Adventures of Huckleberry Finn), Robert B. Sherman and Richard M. Sherman
Cast
Jeff East – Huckleberry Finn
Paul Winfield – Jim
Harvey Korman – The King
David Wayne – The Duke
Arthur O'Connell – Col. Grangerford
Gary Merrill – Pap
Natalie Trundy – Mrs. Loftus
Lucille Benson – Widder Douglas
Kim O'Brien – Maryjane Wilks
Jean Fay – Susan Wilks
Ruby Leftwich – Miss Watson
Produced by Robert Greenhut
Original music by Richard M. Sherman (songs)
Cinematography by Laszlo Kovacs
Film Editing by Michael F. Anderson

36. *Shampoo* (1975)

Satire of Southern California lifestyles with Warren Beatty as promiscuous hairdresser. Carrie Fisher's screen debut. Five Academy Award nominations; Lee Grant won Best Supporting Actress.

Directed by Hal Ashby
Writing credits – Robert Towne and Warren Beatty

Cast
Warren Beatty – George Roundy
Julie Christie – Jackie Shawn
Goldie Hawn – Jill
Lee Grant – Felicia
Jack Warden – Lester
Tony Bill – Johnny Pope
George Furth – Mr. Pettis
Jay Robinson – Norman
Ann Weldon – Mary
Luana Anders – Devra
Randy Scheer – Dennis
Susanna Moore – Gloria
Carrie Fisher – Lorna
Mike Olton – Ricci
Richard E. Kalk – Detective Younger
Ronald Dunas – Nate
Hal Buckley – Kenneth
Jack Bernardi – Izzy

William Castle – Sid Roth
Produced by Warren Beatty
Original music by Paul Simon
Cinematography by Laszlo Kovacs
Film Editing by Robert C. Jones

37. *At Long Last Love* (1975)

Peter Bogdanovich's Cole Porter musical with live singing and dancing.

Directed by Peter Bogdanovich
Writing credits – Peter Bogdanovich

Cast
Burt Reynolds – Michael Oliver Pritchard III
Cybill Shepherd – Brooke Carter
Madeline Kahn – Kitty O'Kelly
Duilio Del Prete – Johnny Spanish
Eileen Brennan – Elizabeth
John Hillerman – Rodney James
Mildred Natwick – Mabel Pritchard
Quinn K. Redeker – Kitty's boyfriend
J. Edward McKinley – Billings
John Stephenson – Abbott
Peter Dane – Williams
William Paterson – Murray
Lester Dorr – Doorman
Liam Dunn – Harry
M. Emmet Walsh – Harold
Produced by Peter Bogdanovich
Music by Cole Porter
Cinematography by Laszlo Kovacs
Film Editing by Douglas Robertson

38. *Nickelodeon* (1976)

Affectionate homage to early days of moviemaking. Ryan O'Neal bumbling into job as director and Burt Reynolds as silent film star.

Directed by Peter Bogdanovich
Writing credits – Peter Bogdanovich, W.D. Richter

Cast
Ryan O'Neal – Leo Harrigan
Burt Reynolds – Buck Greenway
Tatum O'Neal – Alice Forsyte
Brian Keith – H.H. Cobb
Stella Stevens – Marty Reeves
John Ritter – Franklin
Frank Jane Hitchcock – Kathleen Cooke
Jack Perkins – Michael Gilhooley
Brion James – Bailiff
Sidney Armus – Judge
Joe Warfield – Defense Attorney
Tamar Cooper – Edna Mae Gilhooley
Alan Gibbs – Patents Hooligan
Mathew Anden – Hecky
Lorenzo Music – Mullins
Produced by Robert Chartoff, Frank Marshall, Irwin Winkler
Original music by Richard Hazard
Cinematography by Laszlo Kovacs
Film Editing by William C. Carruth (as William Carruth)

39. *Harry and Walter Go to New York* (1976)

Turn-of-the-century (20th) crime comedy about two vaudeville performers hired by British businessman to pull a caper.

Directed by Mark Rydell
Writing credits – John Byrum, Don Devlin, Robert Kaufman

Cast
James Caan – Harry Dighby
Elliott Gould – Walter Hill
Michael Caine – Adam Worth
Diane Keaton – Lissa Chestnut
Charles Durning – Rufus T. Crisp
Lesley Ann Warren – Gloria Fontaine
Val Avery – Chatsworth
Jack Gilford – Mischa
Dennis Dugan – Lewis
Carol Kane – Florence
Kathryn Grody – Barbara
David Proval – Ben
Michael Conrad – Billy Gallagher
Burt Young – Warden Durgom
Bert Remsen – Guard O'Meara
Produced by Tony Bill
Original music by Alan Bergman. Marilyn Bergman, David Shire

Cinematography by Laszlo Kovacs
Film Editing by David Bretherton, Don Guidice, Monte Hellman (uncredited additional editing)

40. *Baby Blue Marine* (1976)

Mistaken identity makes a Marine dropout a WWII hero to residents of a small town.

Directed by John D. Hancock
Writing credits – Stanford Whitmore

Cast
Jan Michael Vincent – Marion
Glynnis O'Connor – Rose
Katherine Helmond – Mrs. Hudkins
Dana Elcar – Sheriff Wenzel
Bert Remsen – Mr. Hudkins
Bruno Kirby – Pop Mosley (as B. Kirby Jr.)
Richard Gere – Raider
Art Lund – Mr. Elmore
Michael Conrad – Drill Instructor
Allan Miller – Capt. Bittman
Produced by Leonard Goldberg and Aaron Spelling
Original music by Fred Karlin
Cinematography by Laszlo Kovacs
Film Editing by Marion Rothman

41. *New York, New York* (1977)

A shimmering homage to the Big Band era that stars Robert DeNiro as a saxophonist and Liza Minnelli as the singer on whom he sets his sights. Lots of great musical numbers, especially the now-famous title song. Director's cut includes "Happy Endings," a lavish number cut from original release.

Directed by Martin Scorsese
Writing credits – Earl Mac Rauch, Mardik Martin

Cast
Liza Minnelli – Francine Evans
Robert De Niro – Jimmy Doyle
Lionel Stander – Tony Harwell
Barry Primus – Paul Wilson
Mary Kay Place – Bernice
Georgie Auld – Frankie Harte
George Memmoli – Nicky
Dick Miller – Palm Club Owner
Murray Moston – Horace Morris
Lenny Gaines – Artie Kirks
Clarence Clemons – Cecil Powell
Kathi McGinnis – Ellen Flannery
Norman Palmer – Desk Clerk
Adam David Winkler – Jimmy Doyle Jr.
Produced by Robert Chartoff, Gene Kirkwood, Irwin Winkler
Original music by Fred Ebb, John Kander, arrangements by Ralph Burns
Cinematography by Laszlo Kovacs
Film Editing by Bert Lovitt (as B. Lovitt), David Ramirez, Tom Rolf

42. *F.I.S.T.* (1978)

Sylvester Stallone as young truck driver who rises to top of the union with help of gangsters.

Directed by Norman Jewison
Writing credits – Joe Eszterhas (story) Joe Eszterhas and Sylvester Stallone

Cast
Sylvester Stallone – Johnny Kovak
Rod Steiger – Senator Andrew Madison
Peter Boyle – Max Graham
Melinda Dillon – Anna Zerinkas
David Huffman – Abe Belkin
Kevin Conway – Vince Doyle
Tony Lo Bianco – Babe Milano
Cassie Yates – Molly Story
Peter Donat – Arthur St. Claire
John Lehne – Mr. Gant
Henry Wilcoxon – Win Talbot
Richard Herd – Mike Monahan
Tony Mockus Jr. – Tom Higgins
Ken Kercheval – Bernie Marr
Elena Karam – Mrs. Zernikas
Joe Tornatore – Angel
James Karen – Andrews
Stuart Gillard – Phil Talbot
Brian Dennehy – Frank Vasko
Produced by Gene Corman, Norman Jewison
Original music by Bill Conti
Cinematography by Laszlo Kovacs
Film Editing by Graeme Clifford

43. *Paradise Alley* (1978)

Three brothers escape from Hell's Kitchen by entering the world of professional wrestling. Sylvester Stallone does it all in this one, including singing the title song.

Directed by Sylvester Stallone
Writing credits – Sylvester Stallone

Cast
Sylvester Stallone – Cosmo Carboni
Lee Canalito – Victor
Armand Assante – Lenny
Frank McRae – Big Glory
Anne Archer – Annie
Kevin Conway – Stitch
Terry Funk – Frankie the Thumper
Joyce Ingalls – Bunchie
Joe Spinell – Burp
Aimée Eccles – Susan Chow
Tom Waits – Mumbles
Chick Casey
Produced by Arthur Chobanian, Edward R. Pressman
Original music by Bill Conti
Cinematography by Laszlo Kovacs
Film Editing by Eve Newman

44. *Runner Stumbles, The* (1979)

Based on the true story of a priest who murdered the nun he fell in love with in a mining town of the 1920s.

Directed by Stanley Kramer
Writing credits – Milan Stitt

Cast
Dick Van Dyke – Father Rivard
Kathleen Quinlan – Sister Rita
Maureen Stapleton – Mrs. Shandig
Ray Bolger – Monsignor Nicholson
Tammy Grimes – Erna
Beau Bridges – Toby
Allen Nause – Prosecutor
John Procaccino – Amos
Produced by Stanley Kramer
Original music by Ernest Gold
Cinematography by Laszlo Kovacs
Film Editing by Pembroke J. Herring

45. *Butch and Sundance: The Early Days* (1979)

Origins of the two famous outlaws, recounted with lots of action.

Directed by Richard Lester
Writing credits Allan Burns

Cast
William Katt – Sundance Kid
Tom Berenger – Butch Cassidy
Jeff Corey – Sheriff Bledsoe
John Schuck – Harvey Logan
Michael C. Gwynne – Mike Cassidy
Peter Weller – Joe Le Fors
Brian Dennehy – O.C. Hanks
Christopher – Bill Carver (as Chris Lloyd)
Jill Eikenberry – Mary
Joel Fluellen – Jack
Regina Baff – Ruby
Peter Brocco – Old Robber
Vincent Schiavelli – Guard
Produced by Steven Bach
Original music by Patrick Williams
Cinematography by Laszlo Kovacs
Film Editing by George Trirogoff

46. *Inside Moves* (1980)

Several handicapped individuals try to cope with life.

Directed by Richard Donner
Writing credits – Valerie Curtin, Barry Levinson, Todd Walton (novel)

Cast
John Savage – Roary
David Morse – Jerry Maxwell
Diana Scarwid – Louise
Amy Wright – Anne
Tony Burton – Lucius Porter
Bill Henderson – 'Blue' Lewis
Steve Kahan – Burt
Jack O'Leary – Max Willatowski

Bert Remsen – 'Stinky'
Harold Russell – 'Wings'
Pepe Serna – Herrada
Harold Sylvester – Alvin Martin
Arnold Williams – Benny
George Brenlin – Cal
Gerri Dean – Hooker
Produced by R.W. Goodwin., Mark M. Tanz
Original music by John Barry
Cinematography by Laszlo Kovacs
Film Editing by Frank Morriss

47. *Heart Beat* (1980)

The lives of the Beat poets, based on Carolyn Cassady's autobiography. Good acting carries the story.

Directed by John Byrum
Writing credits – Carolyn Cassady (autobiography), John Byrum

Cast
Nick Nolte – Neal Cassady
Sissy Spacek – Carolyn Cassady
John Heard – Jack Kerouac
Ray Sharkey – Ira
Ann Dusenberry – Stevie
Margaret Fairchild – Mrs. Kerouac
Tony Bill – Dick
Mary Margaret Amato – Waitress
Kent Williams – Ogden
Susan Niven – Ogden's Secretary
Marcia Nasatir – First Receptionist
Mickey Kelly – Second Receptionist
Luis Contreras – Mexican Junkie
Produced by David Axelrod, Alan Greisman, Edward R. Pressman, Michael Shamberg
Original music by Jack Nitzsche
Cinematography by Laszlo Kovacs
Film Editing by Eric Jenkins

48. *Legend of the Lone Ranger, The* (1981)

The origin of the Lone Ranger and how he teamed up with Tonto is told with vivid cinematography. Narrated by Merle Haggard.

Directed by William A. Fraker
Writing credits – Ivan Goff, William Roberts, George W. Trendle (characters)

Cast
Klinton Spilsbury – The Lone Ranger
Michael Horse – Tonto
Christopher Lloyd – Cavandish
Matt Clark – Sheriff Wiatt
Juanin Clay – Amy Striker
Jason Robards Jr. – President Ulysses S. Grant
John Bennett Perry – Dan Reid
John Hart – Lucas Striker
Richard Farnsworth – Wild Bill Hickok
Lincoln Tate – General Custer
Ted Flicker – Buffalo Bill Cody
Produced by Walter Coblenz, Lew Grade, Martin Starger
Original music by John Barry
Cinematography by Laszlo Kovacs
Film Editing by Thomas Stanford

49. *Toy, The* (1982)

Hard-luck newspaper reporter becomes new "toy" of spoiled child.

Directed by Richard Donner
Writing credits – Carol Sobieski, Francis Veber (book)

Cast
Richard Pryor – Jack Brown
Jackie Gleason – U. S. Bates
Ned Beatty – Mr. Morehouse
Scott Schwartz – Eric Bates
Teresa Ganzel – Fancy Bates
Wilfrid Hyde—White
Barkley Annazette Chase – Angela
Tony King – Clifford
Don Hood – O'Brien
Karen Leslie —Lyttle Fräulein
Virginia Capers – Ruby Simpson
Produced by Jeffrey Benjamin, Ray Stark
Original music by Trevor Lawrence (songs), Frank Musker (songs), Patrick Williams
Cinematography by Laszlo Kovacs
Film Editing by Richard A. Harris (as Richard Harris), Michael A. Stevenson

50. *Frances* (1982)

Story of troubled actress Frances Farmer and her turbulent journey through Hollywood in 1930s and '40s. Great visual poetry and Oscar-nominated performances by Jessica Lange and Kim Stanley.

Directed by Graeme Clifford
Writing credits – Eric Bergren, Christopher De Vore, Nicholas Kazan

Cast
Jessica Lange – Frances Farmer
Kim Stanley – Lillian Farmer
Sam Shepard – Harry York
Bart Burns – Ernest Farmer
Jonathan Banks – Hitchhiker
Bonnie Bartlett – Stylist
James Brodhead – Sergeant
Jane Jenkins – Lady at Roosevelt Hotel (as J.J. Chaback)
Jordan Charney – Harold Clurman
Rod Colbin – Sentencing Judge
Daniel Chodos – Director
Donald Craig – Ralph Edwards
Jeffrey DeMunn – Clifford Odets
Produced by Mel Brooks
Original music by John Barry
Cinematography by Laszlo Kovacs
Film Editing by John Wright

51. *Ghostbusters* (1984)

Blockbuster comedy about team of paranormal investigators fighting ghosts taking over New York. Zany characters and great special effects. A sequel was released in 1989.

Directed by Ivan Reitman
Writing credits – Dan Aykroyd & Harold Ramis

Cast
Bill Murray Dr. – Peter Venkman
Dan Aykroyd – Dr. Raymond Stantz
Sigourney Weaver – Dana Barrett/Zuul (the Gate Keeper)
Harold Ramis – Dr. Egon Spengler
Rick Moranis – Louis Tully/Vinz Clortho (the Key Master)
Annie Potts – Janine Melnitz
William Atherton – Walter Peck
Ernie Hudson – Winston Zeddemore
David Margulies – Mayor
Steven Tash – Male Student
Jennifer Runyon – Jennifer
Slavitza Jovan – Gozer
Produced by Bernie Brillstein, Michael C. Gross, Joe Medjuck, Ivan Reitman
Original music by Elmer Bernstein, Ray Parker Jr. (song)
Cinematography by Laszlo Kovacs
Film Editing by David E. Blewitt (as David Blewit), Sheldon Kahn

52. *Crackers* (1984)

Two bungling thieves go on a crime spree in this offbeat comedy, a remake of *Big Deal on Madonna Street.*

Directed by Louis Malle
Writing credits – Jeffrey Alan Fiskin

Cast
Donald Sutherland – Weslake
Jack Warden – Garvey
Sean Penn – Dillard
Wallace Shawn – Turtle
Larry Riley – Boardwalk
Trinidad Silva – Ramon
Christine Baranski – Maxine
Charlayne Woodard – Jasmine
Tasia Valenza – Maria
Irwin Corey – Lazzarelli
Edouard DeSoto – Don Fernando
Produced by Edward Lewis
Original music by Paul Chihara
Cinematography by Laszlo Kovacs
Film Editing by Suzanne Baron

53. *Mask* (1985)

Heartfelt film about a teenager afflicted with elephantiasis who overcomes his condition and takes his place in world of California bikers.

Directed by Peter Bogdanovich
Writing credits – Anna Hamilton Phelan

Cast
Cher – Francais 'Rusty' Dennis
Sam Elliott – Gar
Eric Stoltz – Roy 'Rocky' Dennis
Estelle Getty – Evelyn
Richard A. – Dysart – Abe
Laura Dern – Diana
Micole Mercurio – Babe
Harry Carey Jr. – Red
Dennis Burkley – Dozer
Lawrence Monoson – Ben
Ben Piazza – Mr. Simms
L. Craig King – Eric
Alexandra Powers – Lisa
Kelly Jo Minter – Lorrie (as Kelly Minter)
Joe Unger – 1st Boyfriend
Todd Allen – Canuck
Howard Hirdler – Stickman
Produced by Martin Starger
Original music by Dennis Ricotta
Cinematography by Laszlo Kovacs
Film Editing by Barbara Ford, Éva Gárdos

54. *Legal Eagles* (1986)

Complicated tale of romance and murder that attempts to incorporate the world of performance art into a mystery.

Directed by Ivan Reitman
Writing credits – Jim Cash, Jack Epps Jr. and Ivan Reitman (story)

Cast
Robert Redford – Tom Logan
Debra Winger – Laura Kelly
Daryl Hannah – Chelsea Deardon
Brian Dennehy – Cavanaugh –
Terence Stamp – Victor Taft
Steven Hill – Bower
David Clennon – Blanchard
John McMartin – Forrester
Jennifer Dundas – Jennifer Logan (as Jennie Dundas)
Roscoe Lee Browne – Judge Dawkins
Christine Baranski – Carol Freeman
Produced by Arne Glimcher, Michael C. Gross, Sheldon Kahn, Joe Medjuck, Ivan Reitman
Original music by Elmer Bernstein
Cinematography by Laszlo Kovacs
Film Editing by William D. Gordean, Pembroke J. Herring, Sheldon Kahn

55. *Little Nikita* (1988)
... aka Sleepers, The (1988)

A California boy discovers his parents are spies. Sidney Poitier is FBI agent on the trail.

Directed by Richard Benjamin
Writing credits – Bo Goldman, John Hill, Tom Musca (story) Terry Schwartz (story)

Cast
Sidney Poitier – Roy Parmenter
River Phoenix – Jeff Grant
Richard Jenkins – Richard Grant
Caroline Kava – Elizabeth Grant
Richard Bradford – Konstantin Karpov
Richard Lynch – Scuba
Loretta Devine – Verna McLaughlin
Lucy Deakins – Barbara Kerry
Jerry Hardin – Brewer
Albert Fortell – Bunin
Ronald Guttman – Spessky
Jacob Vargas – Miguel
Roberto Jiménez – Joaquin
Robb Madrid – Sergeant Leathers
Produced by Harry Gittes, Art Levinson, Gail Mutrux
Original music by Marvin Hamlisch
Cinematography by Laszlo Kovacs
Film Editing by Jacqueline Cambas

56. *Say Anything...* (1989)

Popular teen romance starring John Cusack as the class oddball who tries to win over the class brain (Ione Skye). Cameron Crowe's directing debut.

Directed by Cameron Crowe
Writing credits (WGA) – Cameron Crowe (written by)

Cast
John Cusack – Lloyd Dobler
Ione Skye – Diane Court

John Mahoney – James Court
Lili Taylor – Corey Flood
Amy Brooks – D.C.
Pamela Segall – Rebecca
Jason Gould – Mike Cameron
Loren Dean – Joe
Glenn Walker Harris Jr. – Jason, Lloyd's Nephew
Charles Walker – Principal
Russel Lunday – Parent
Polly Platt – Mrs. Flood
Gloria Cromwell – Ruth
Joan Cusack – Constance Dobler (uncredited)
Produced by James L. Brooks, Paul Germain, Richard Marks, Polly Platt
Original music by Walter Becker
Cinematography by Laszlo Kovacs
Film Editing by Richard Marks

57. *Shattered* (1991)

... aka Plastic Nightmare (1991) (Belgium: English title)

As he recovers from an automobile accident, an architect's memory gradually returns – and his memories include adultery and murder.

Directed by Wolfgang Petersen
Writing credits (WGA) – Richard Neely (novel), Wolfgang Petersen (screenplay)

Cast
Tom Berenger – Dan Merrick
Bob Hoskins – Gus Klein
Greta Scacchi – Judith Merrick
Joanne Whalley – Jenny Scott (as Joanne Whalley—Kilmer)
Corbin Bernsen – Jeb Scott
Debi A. Monahan – Nancy Mercer
Bert Rosario – Rudy Costa
Jedda Jones – Sadie
Scott Getlin – Jack Stanton
Kellye Nakahara – Lydia
Donna Hardy – Pet Shop Woman
Frank Cavestani – Cop
Produced by John Davis
Original music by Ashley Irwin (additional music) Alan Silvestri
Cinematography by Laszlo Kovacs
Film Editing by Glenn Farr , Hannes Nikel

58. *Radio Flyer* (1992)

When their mother marries an abusive alcoholic, two boys take refuge in a world of fantasy. Imaginative treatment of difficult subject matter.

Directed by Richard Donner
Writing credits (WGA) – David Mickey Evans

Cast
Lorraine Bracco – Mary
John Heard – Daugherty
Adam Baldwin – The King
Elijah Wood – Mike
Joseph Mazzello – Bobby
Ben Johnson – Geronimo Bill
Sean Baca – Fisher
Robert Munic – Older Fisher
Garette Ratliff Henson – Chad
Thomas Ian Nicholas – Ferdie
Noah Verduzco – Victor Hernandez
Isaac Ocampo – Jorge Hernandez
Kaylan Romero – Jesus Hernandez
Abraham Verduzco – Carlos Hernandez
T.J. Evans – Big Raymond
Victor DiMattia – Little Raymond
Produced by Rick Bieber
Original music by Hans Zimmer
Cinematography by Laszlo Kovacs
Film Editing by Stuart Baird, Dallas Puett

59. *Ruby Cairo* (1993)

... aka Deception (1993)
... aka Missing Link: Ruby Cairo, The (1993)

Mystery about a resolute woman who travels around the world locating different bank accounts of her deceased spouse.

Directed by Graeme Clifford
Writing credits (WGA) – Robert Dillon (story and screenplay) and Michael Thomas (screenplay)

Cast
Andie MacDowell – Bessie Faro
Liam Neeson – Fergus Lamb
Viggo Mortensen – Johnny Faro

Jack Thompson – Ed
Paul Spencer – Johnny Faro (Boy)
Chad Power – Niles Faro
Monica Mikala – Alexandria Faro
Kaelynn Craddick – Cleo Faro
Sara Craddick – Cleo Faro
Luis Cortés – Hermes #1
Amy Van Nostrand – Marge
Produced by Haruki Kadokawa
Original music by John Barry, Robert Randles (ethnic music)
Cinematography by Laszlo Kovacs
Film Editing by Caroline Biggerstaff, Paul Rubell

60. *Next Karate Kid, The* (1994)

Fourth sequel in the series, with Pat Morita training tomboy Hilary Swank, daughter of an old wartime pal who once saved his life.

Directed by Christopher Cain
Writing credits (WGA) – Robert Mark Kamen (characters), Mark Lee (written by)

Cast
Pat Morita – Sergeant Kesuke 'Miyagi—San' Miyagi (as Noriyuki "Pat" Morita)
Hilary Swank – Julie 'Julie—San' Pierce
Michael Ironside – Colonel Dugan
Constance Towers – Louisa 'Louisa—San' Pierce
Chris Conrad – Eric McGowen
Arsenio 'Sonny' Trinidad – Abbot Monk (as Arsenio Trinidad)
Michael Cavalieri – Ned
Walt Goggins – Charlie
Jim Ishida – Tall Monk
Rodney Kageyama – Monk
Seth Sakai – Buddist Monk
Eugene Boles – Mr. Harold Wilkes
Keena Keel – School Clerk
Produced by Jerry Weintraub
Original music by Bill Conti, Dolores O'Riordan (song)
Cinematography by Laszlo Kovacs
Film Editing by Ronald Roose

61. *Scout, The* (1994)

Sports comedy/drama with Albert Brooks as down-on-his-luck scout who finds backwoods phenomenon Brendan Fraser. Yankee owner George Steinbrenner plays himself.

Directed by Michael Ritchie
Writing credits (WGA) Roger Angell (article), Andrew Bergman (screenplay) and Albert Brooks (screenplay), Monica Mcgowan Johnson

Cast
Albert Brooks – Al Percolo
Brendan Fraser – Steve Nebraska
Dianne Wiest – Doctor H. Aaron
Anne Twomey – Jennifer
Lane Smith – Ron Wilson
MichaelRapaport – Tommy Lacy
Barry Shabaka Henley – McDermott
John Capodice – Caruso
Louis Giovannetti – World Series Catcher
Stephen Demek— Yankee Catcher
Ralph Drischell – Charlie
Brett Rickaby – George's Assistant
Produced by Jack Cummings
Original music by Bill Conti
Cinematography by Laszlo Kovacs (as Laszlo Kovacs)
Film Editing by Pembroke J. Herring, Don Zimmerman

62. *Free Willy 2: The Adventure Home* (1995)

Jesse is reunited with his deep-sea pal while camping in Pacific Northwest.

Directed by Dwight H. Little
Writing credits (WGA) Keith A. Walker (characters) Karen Janszen, Corey Blechman, John Mattson

Cast
Jason James Richter – Jesse
Francis Capra – Elvis
Mary Kate Schellhardt – Nadine
August Schellenberg – Randolph Johnson
Michael Madsen – Glen Greenwood

Jayne Atkinson – Annie Greenwood
Mykelti Williamson – Dwight Mercer
Elizabeth Peña – Kate Haley
Jon Tenney – John Milner
Paul Tuerpe – Milner's Assistant
M. Emmet Walsh – Wilcox
John Considine – Commander Blake
Steve Kahan – Captain Nilson
Neal Matarazzo – Helmsman Kelly
Al Sapienza – Engineer
Produced by Richard Donner
Original music by Michael Jackson (song) Basil Poledouris
Cinematography by Laszlo Kovacs
Film Editing by Robert Brown, Dallas Puett

63. *Copycat* (1995)

Jailed serial killer helps psychologist Sigourney Weaver and detective Holly Hunter track a copycat killer.

Directed by Jon Amiel
Writing credits – Ann Biderman, David Madsen (II)

Cast
Sigourney Weaver – Helen Hudson
Holly Hunter – M.J. Monahan
Dermot Mulroney – Reuben Goetz
William McNamara – Peter Foley
Harry Connick Jr. – Daryll Lee Cullum
J.E. Freeman – Lt. Quinn
Will Patton – Nicoletti
John Rothman – Andy
Shannon O'Hurley – Susan Schiffer
Produced by Joseph M. Caracciolo Jr., Arnon Milchan Mark Tarlov
Original music by Gabriel Fauré
Cinematography by Laszlo Kovacs
Film Editing by Jim Clark, Alan Heim

64. *Multiplicity* (1996)

Overworked Michael Keaton clones wildly varying versions of himself.

Directed by Harold Ramis
Writing credits – Chris Miller (short story and screenplay), Mary Hale, Lowell Ganz, Babaloo Mandel

Cast
Michael Keaton – Doug Kinney
Andie MacDowell – Laura Kinney
Zack Duhame – Zack Kinney
Katie Schlossberg – Jennifer Kinney
Harris Yulin – Dr. Leeds
Richard Masur – Del King
Eugene Levy – Vic
Ann Cusack – Noreen
John de Lancie – Ted
Judith Kahan – Franny
Brian Doyle—Murray – Walt
Obba Babatundé – Paul
Produced by Trevor Albert, Harold Ramis
Original music by George Fenton
Cinematography by Laszlo Kovacs
Film Editing by Craig Herring, Pembroke J. Herring (as Pem Herring)

65. *My Best Friend's Wedding* (1997)

Julia Roberts plots to foil best friend's upcoming wedding because she thinks she's in love with him.

Directed by P.J. Hogan
Writing credits – Ronald Bass

Cast
Julia Roberts – Julianne 'Jules' Potter
Dermot Mulroney – Michael 'Mike' O'Neal
Cameron Diaz – Kimberly 'Kim/Kimmy' Wallace
Rupert Everett – George Downes
Philip Bosco – Walter Wallace
M. Emmet Walsh – Joe O'Neal
Rachel Griffiths – Samantha Newhouse
Carrie Preston – Mandy Newhouse
Produced by Ronald Bass, Jerry Zucker
Original music by Burt Bacharach (songs), James Newton Howard
Cinematography by Laszlo Kovacs
Film Editing by Garth Craven, Lisa Fruchtman

66. *Jack Frost* (1998)

... aka Frost (1998)

Workaholic dies in auto accident and is

reincarnated as a snowman to comfort his son and wife.

Directed by Troy Miller
Writing credits – Mark Steven Johnson and Steven Bloom

Cast
Michael Keaton – Jack Frost
Kelly Preston – Gabby Frost
Joseph Cross – Charlie Frost
Mark Addy – Mac MacArthur
Andrew Lawrence – Tuck Gronic (as Andy Lawrence)
Eli Marienthal – Spencer
Will Rothhaar – Dennis
Mika Boorem – Natalie
Benjamin Brock – Alexander
Taylor Handley – Rory Buck
Joe Rokicki – Mitch
Cameron Ferre – Pudge
Ahmet Zappa – Snowplow Driver
Paul F. Tompkins – Audience Member
Henry Rollins – Sid Gronic
Dweezil Zappa – John Kaplan
Produced by Irving Azoff
Original music by Michael Keaton (song "Don't Lose Your Faith") Trevor Rabin
Cinematography by Laszlo Kovacs
Film Editing by Lawrence Jordan

66. *Return to Me* (2000)

Romantic comedy set in Chicago. Heartbroken widower David Duchovny falls in love with sheltered Minnie Driver and discovers they have a surprising connection.

Directed by Bonnie Hunt
Writing credits – Bonnie Hunt, Don Lake (story and screenplay), Andrew Stern, Samantha Goodman (story)

Cast
David Duchovny – Bob Rueland
Minnie Driver – Grace Briggs
Carroll O'Connor – Marty O'Reilly
Robert Loggia – Angelo Pardipillo
Bonnie Hunt – Megan Dayton
David Alan Grier – Charlie Johnson
Joely Richardson – Elizabeth Rueland
Eddie Jones – Emmett McFadden
James Belushi – Joe Dayton
Marianne Muellerleile – Sophie
Produced by C.O. Erickson, Jennie Lew Tugend
Original music by Nicholas Pike
Cinematography by Laszlo Kovacs
Film Editing by Garth Craven

67. *Miss Congeniality* (2000)

No-nonsense FBI Agent Sandra Bullock is groomed to go undercover as a beauty-pageant contestant.

Directed by Donald Petrie
Writing credits – Marc Lawrence, Katie Ford, Caryn Lucas

Cast
Sandra Bullock – FBI Agent Grace 'Gracie' Hart/Gracie Lou Freebush ('Miss New Jersey')
Michael Caine – Victor 'Mr. Vic/Vic' Melling
Benjamin Bratt – FBI Agent Eric Matthews/ Eric Bob
Candice Bergen – Kathy Morningside
William Shatner – Stan Fields
Ernie Hudson – FBI Agent Harry McDonald
John DiResta – FBI Agent Clonsky
Heather Burn – Cheryl Frasier ('Miss Rhode Island')
Melissa De Sousa – Karen Krantz ('Miss New York')
Steve Monroe – Frank Tobin/Frank Morningside
Deirdre Quinn – Mary Jo Wright ('Miss Texas')
Wendy Raquel Robinson – Leslie Williams ('Miss California)
Asia De Marcos – Alana Krewson ('Miss Hawaii')
Produced by Bruce Berman, Sandra Bullock, Katie Ford
Original music by Ed Shearmur
Cinematography by Laszlo Kovacs
Film Editing by Billy Weber

INDEX